Data Rookies Labs: Data Mining with Orange

Pattern Discovery with Visual Tools

Data Analytics Curriculum, LLC

About the Publisher

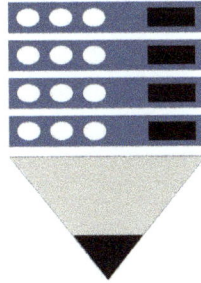

Data Analytics Curriculum

Data Analytics Curriculum, LLC creates approachable, visually engaging educational materials that make data science and technology accessible for learners from high school to college and independent study.

Please see our website or TPT online store for additional titles and resources such as slides, additional book forms, content (non lab) textbooks to accompany these labs, solution guides and other resources to help you teach and learn.

Additional resources available:

Website: https://www.dataanalyticscurriculum.com

Acknowledgement

This book makes use of Orange Data Mining software, developed by the Bioinformatics Laboratory at the University of Ljubljana. Orange is open-source software released under the GNU General Public License v3.

For more information, visit https://orange.biolab.si.

All screenshots, workflows, and examples based on Orange are used in compliance with this license.

Contents

Lab 1

Get Started with Orange

Orange is a free, open-source data mining tool that uses visual programming with Python in the background. It allows you to explore data analysis workflows without writing code. It is available for download at orangedatamining.com.

Because Orange runs on Python you must first have Python installed although Orange guides you through this if it does not detect a prior installation. Orange requires no coding unless advanced usage is intended although it does fully integrate with Python and understand the language.

Note Orange does a base installation. There are additional packages available that need to be installed as add ins for specific tasks (such as Text Analytics or Association Analysis).

1.1   Lesson Steps

Step 1: Starting Orange

When you first launch Orange a Welcome Screen appears.

1

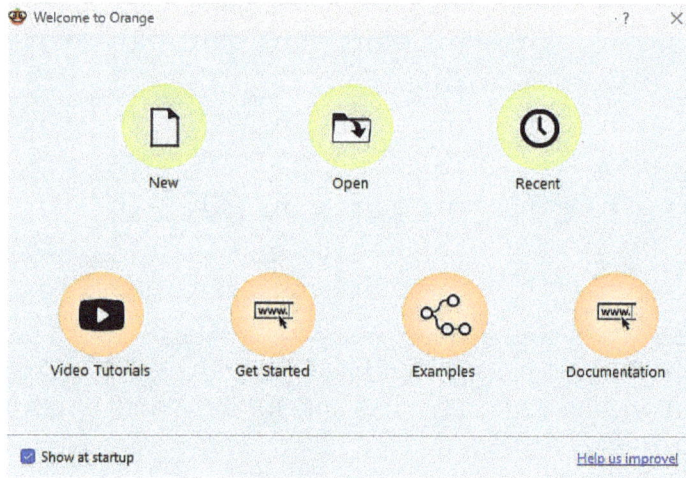

From here you have the options of starting a new workflow, opening a recent (workflow) file, or exploring documentation and tutorials Orange provides online. Select the option to start a new workflow.

Step 2: Orange Interface Overview

Let's get familiar with the Orange environment. There are two main components. On the right is the Canvas area (which is simply a blank white workspace which on start-up has nothing in it). On the left is a widget directory (the left panel). This is where you can obtain the widgets you need and drag and drop them onto the workspace. Note that the widgets are grouped by tasks (Data, Visualize, etc.).

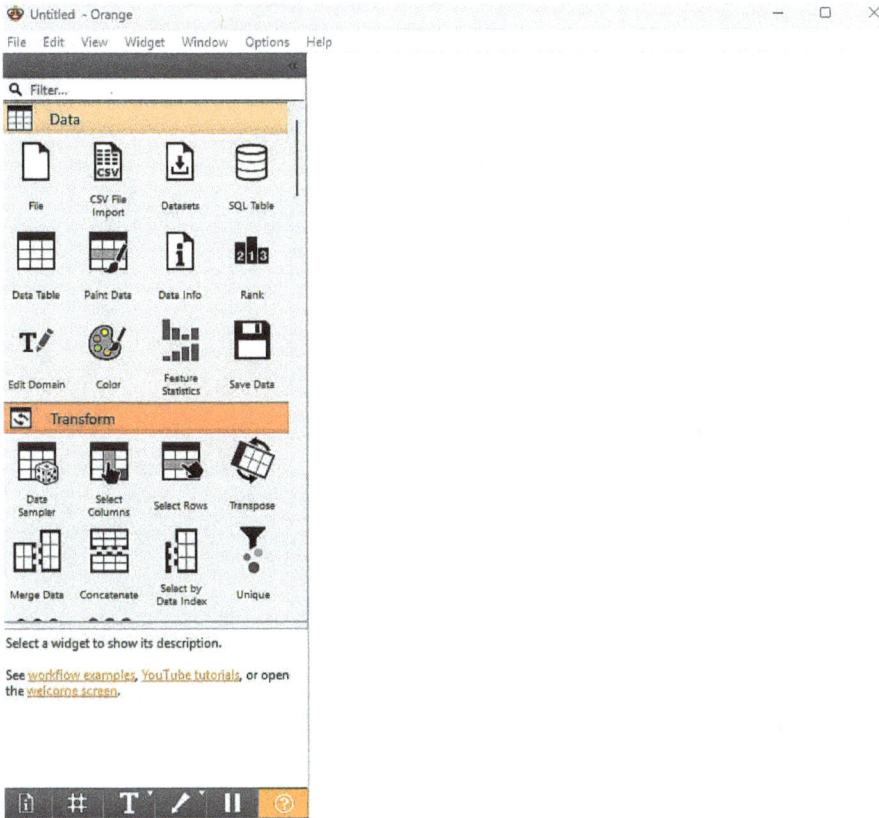

Step 3: Widgets

Widgets are modular tools for tasks like data import, analysis, and visualization. Underneath (and invisible to you) each widget is Python specific programming. When you use widgets you are effectively sending input and receiving output form the underlying Python code, but you do not need to do any coding to use Orange.

As you hover over the widgets it gives details on what each widget does (on the bottom left). Read the descriptions shown. Each widget has a specific role. For example, the File widget loads data from your computer, while Datasets can load example files. Understanding each widget's function helps you choose the right one for your task.

Step 4: Load Sample Data

Now let's create a practice workflow and get you ready to use Orange. Drag a Datasets widget from the Data group onto the Canvas.

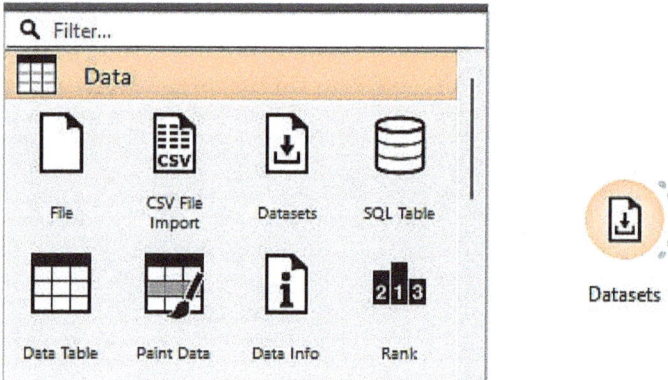

Double-click to open it and select Iris dataset which is built into the system (we are not yet loading external data).

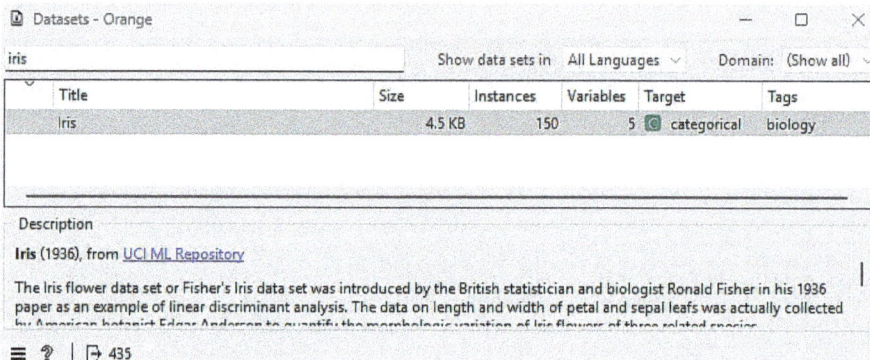

Step 5: View the Data

Add a Data Table widget to the canvas. Connect this to the Datasets widget.

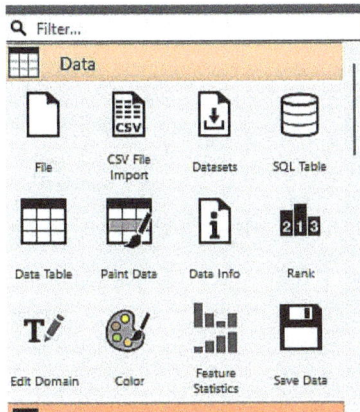

Click on the Data Table widget to view the data.

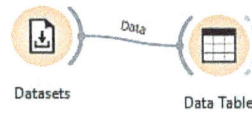

Step 6: Visualize the Data

From the Visualize group, drag a Scatter Plot widget onto the canvas. Connect the Data Table to the Scatter Plot.

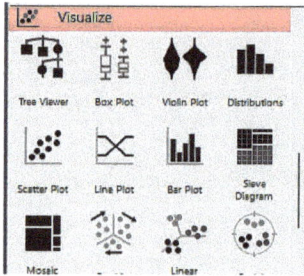

Double-click Scatter Plot to view the graph (play around with the graph axis and settings to explore more).

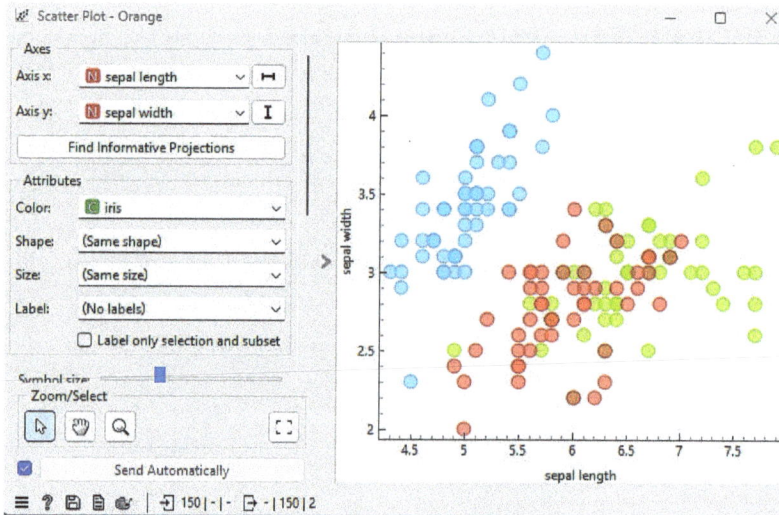

Step 7: Save Your Work

Go to File > Save As. Save the project with a name. Orange saves files as .ows (Orange Workflow Schema). You can also export results or create a journal for sharing.

Very importantly - once a workflow is setup and saved it can be used for different data simply by using a different dataset in the starting widget. This can be very helpful to not always have to start each workflow from scratch.

1.2 Wrap-Up

This lab was introduction to Orange's visual programming environment. It covered how to launch the app, add and connect widgets, load sample data, and view simple visualizations. Orange makes it simple to do analytics and you can build and reuse workflows, and you don't have to write code. Now you are ready to learn NLP.

Lab 2

Exploring Data

Before we can build models or analyze patterns for mining data, we need to explore data itself. In this lab, you'll walk through loading a dataset, examining its structure, and using basic visual tools to get a feel for the data that you are working on. This kind of early exploration helps flag potential issues and gives an overall sense of the data's content, quality, and quirks.

2.1 Lesson Steps

Step 1: Start a New Workflow

Open Orange. Start a new project by creating a Blank Workflow.

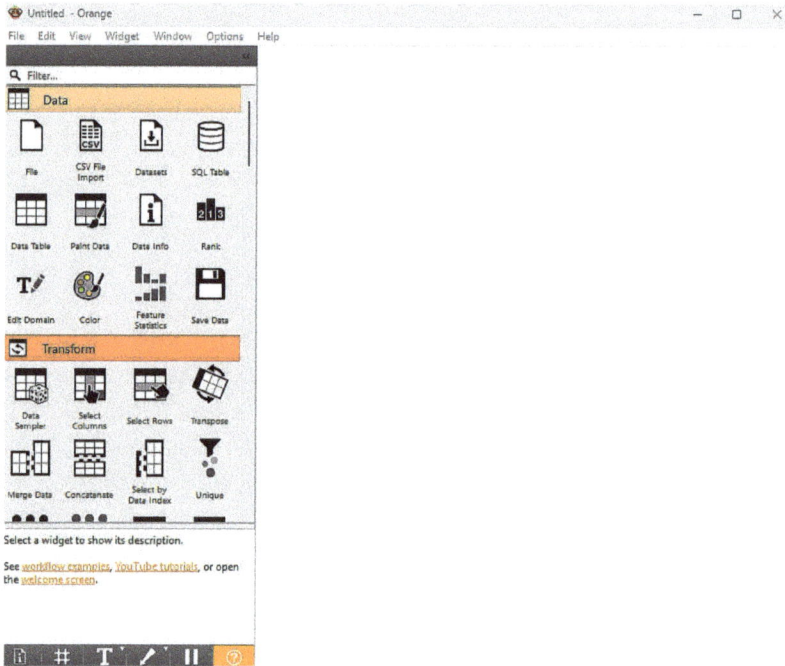

Step 2: Browse the Data Menu

Look at the menu on the left side of the Orange interface and the different
widgets in the Data menu (hover over and on the bottom of the menu area is
a description). This section contains tools for loading, inspecting, and trans-
forming data. These are important for all Orange projects. Only standard
formats like CSV and Excel are supported by Orange. Proprietary formats
(e.g., SAS, SPSS) won't work and you would need to use software to convert
them to CSV or Excel if your data is in that form in order to use your data in
Orange.

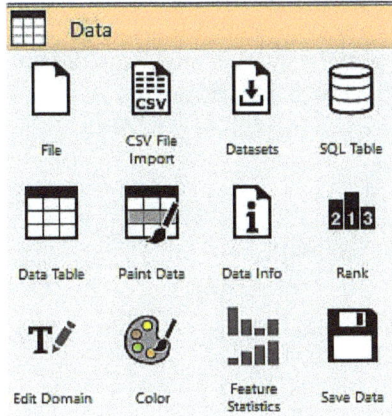

Step 3: Add CSV File Import Widget

Drag a CSV File Import widget onto the workflow canvas from the Data menu. This widget will allow you to load external CSV files

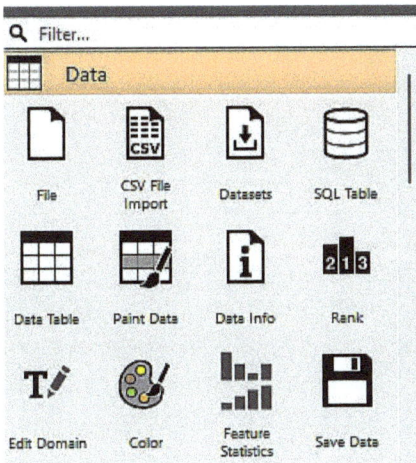

Step 4: Load the Dataset

Double click on the CSV File Import widget you have placed on the canvas. In the popup window, navigate to and select the file tutorial_elNino.csv. This is a dataset related to El Niño weather patterns. This dataset will serve as your playground for this lab exploring Orange's data tools.

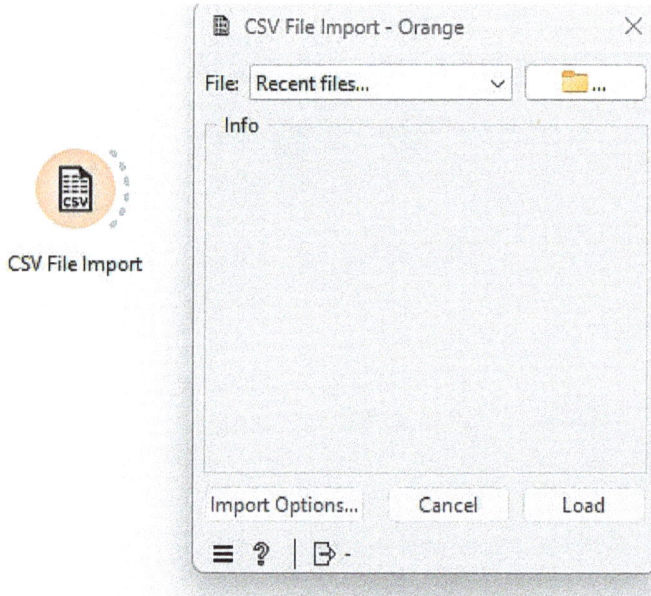

Step 5: Set Import Options

Orange doesn't always guess the correct data types especially when using CSV files (it will often upload CSV files with incorrect types). CSV files have no metadata in them so no information about data types is imported. Manually setting data types ensure your analysis works correctly. For instance, you don't want numeric columns treated as text or vice versa.

After loading the csv file, another window will open for Import Options (can also click on the Import Options button).

Select the column and use the Column Type drop downs to set the correct data types for each column (Numeric, Categorical, or Ignore) as shown.

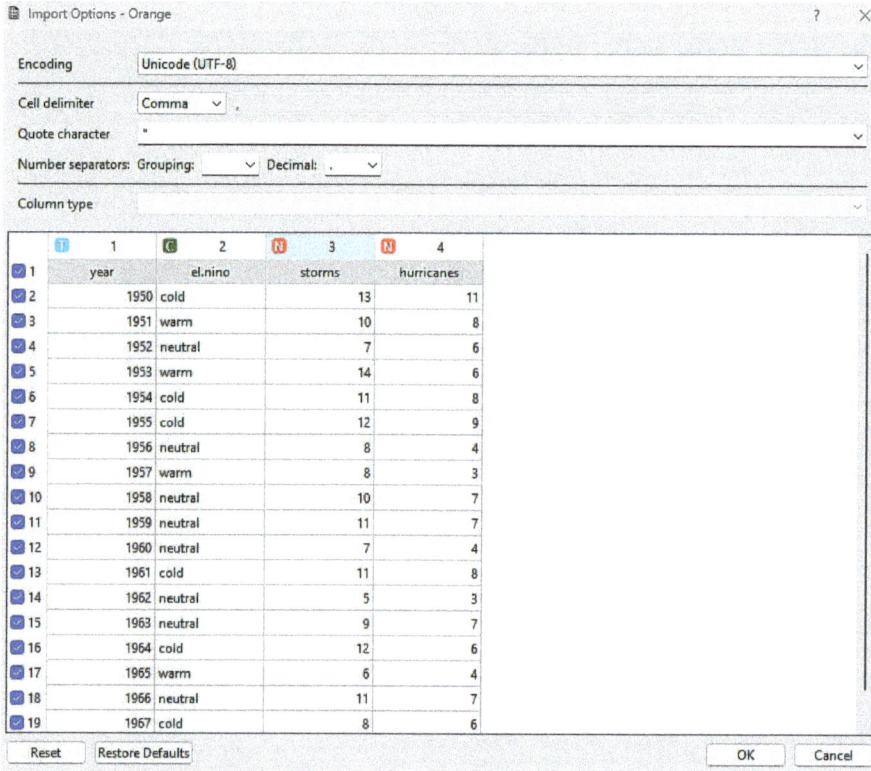

Step 6: View Feature Statistics

A feature in data mining is an individual measurable property or character-
istic of a data instance used for analysis or modeling (and yes this really is a
fancy name for variable). Drag a Feature Statistics widget from the Data menu
onto the canvas. Connect it to the CSV File Import widget.

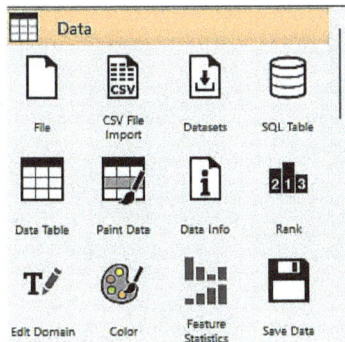

Double-click it to view the output.

The Feature Statistics widget shows basic statistics for each variable—such as mean, min, max, and distribution shape. It's a quick way to understand the structure and quality of your data. Note: Orange is not a full statistical tool and does not have the advanced functionality for statistics that R or SPSS and others have. Very little is customizable in Orange (unlike R or SAS where everything can be coded and customized). However, this widget provides handy summary views for data exploration for pre-data mining screening and understanding data.

Step 7: Explore Distributions

Drag a Distributions widget from the Visualize menu. Connect it to the CSV File Import widget.

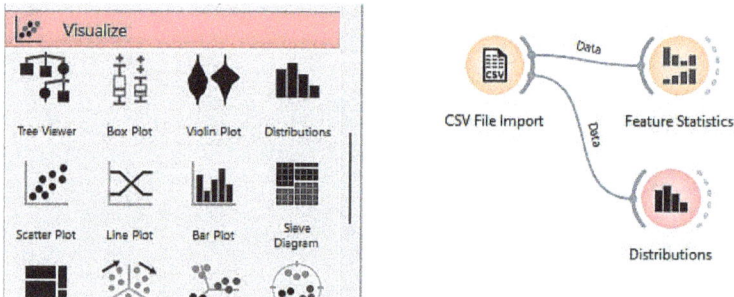

Open the widget and use the filters on the left to explore different variables. Note the bin width adjustor comes in handy for numeric variables.

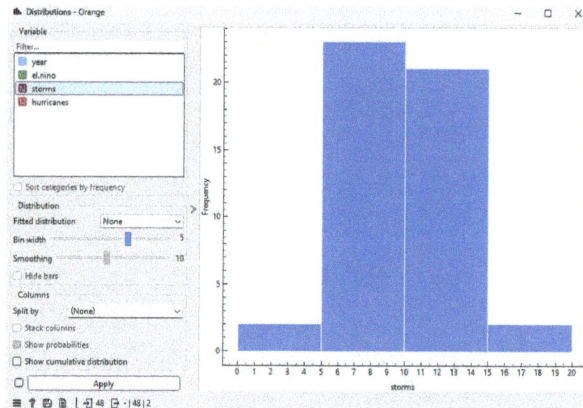

The Distributions widget shows visual plots (like histograms) that help you spot skewed data, gaps, or unusual values. This can be important for making sure there are not issues with the data that can interfere with data mining results.

Step 8: Use a Box Plot

Box plots are great for showing spread of data and outliers. You can compare variables or categories to see which have wider ranges, extreme values, or symmetry or asymmetry of a distribution.

Add a Box Plot widget (from Visualize menu) and connect it to the CSV File Import widget.

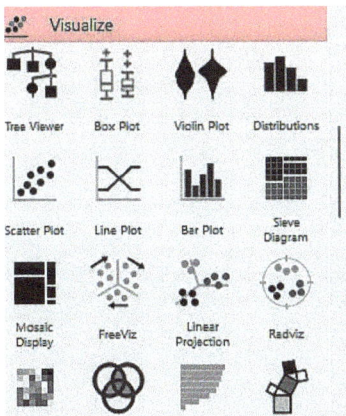

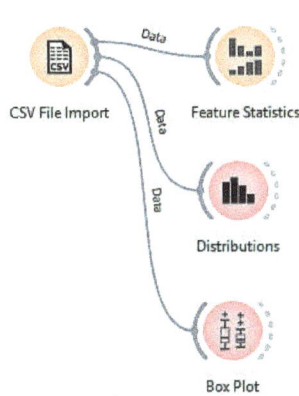

Open the widget and test out the options on the left to view various boxplots and options.

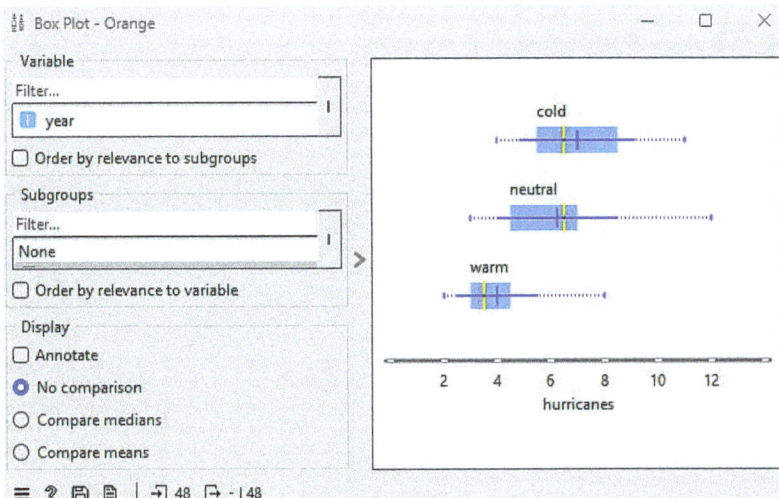

Step 9: Create a Scatter Plot

Scatter plots show relationships between two numeric variables. This is important for looking at trends and correlations in the data. Add a Scatter Plot widget from the Visualize menu and connect it to the CSV File Import widget.

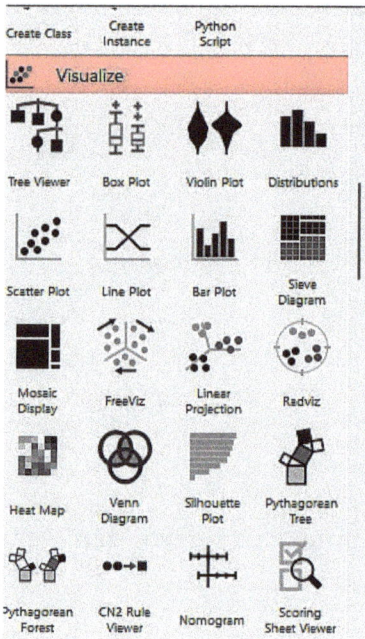

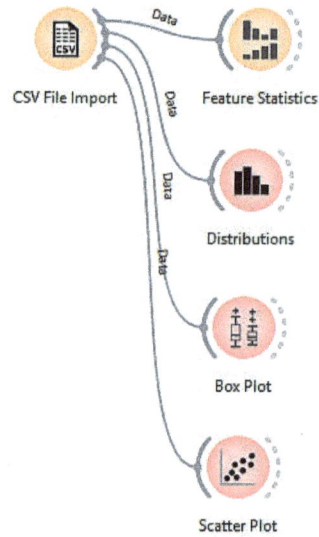

Use it to plot Storms on one axis and Hurricanes on the other and color code the plot by el Nino.

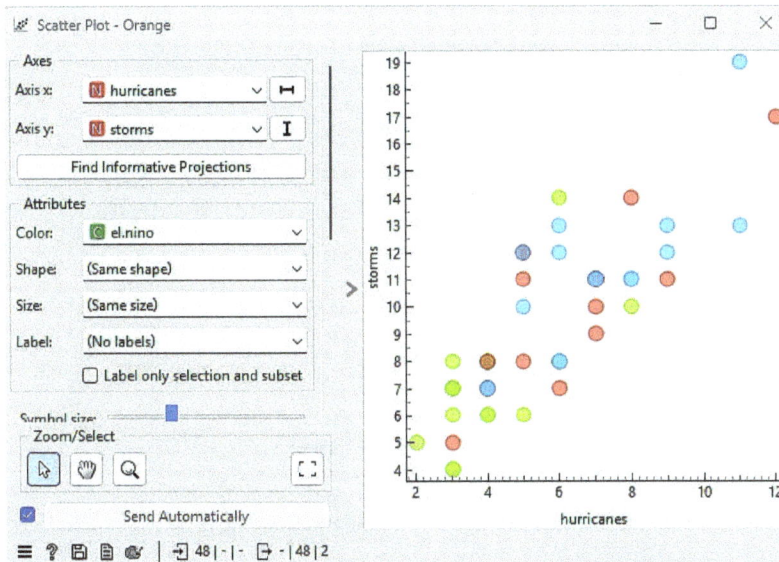

Step 10: Save Your Workflow

Orange saves workflows in a .ows format, which can only be opened in Orange. If you want to save the data, use the Save Data widget from the Data menu to export it as CSV or Excel.

2.2 Wrap-Up

In this lab, you built an Orange workflow, loaded a dataset, and explored it using several visual tools. These steps might seem basic, but they're critical for any data project. Knowing what your data looks like, what kinds of values it contains, and where there might be issues helps you make better decisions later. As you move forward, you'll build on this foundation to do deeper analyses, but every good project starts with knowing your data.

2.3   Exercises

Exploring Data

This lab lets you practice loading, exploring, and visually analyzing real-world datasets using Orange. You will load CSV files, inspect data types, generate basic statistics, and visualize data using distributions, box plots, and scatter plots.

1. Load each CSV dataset into Orange using the CSV File Import widget.
2. Use the Data Table widget to inspect data types and sample values.
3. Generate basic statistics (mean, min, max, variance) with the Feature Statistics widget.
4. Visualize data distributions using Distributions, Box Plot, and Scatter Plot widgets.
5. Explore categorical variables with Bar Charts or Mosaic Plots as appropriate.
6. Analyze relationships between variables by grouping or coloring plots based on categories.
7. Answer all questions by interpreting the widget outputs, including providing text explanations or screenshots.

Dataset 1: Wildlife Sightings

Use the file wildlife_sightings.csv. This dataset tracks wildlife sightings by species, location, and time of day.

1. What are the minimum, maximum, and average values of the Count variable?
2. What is the most frequently sighted Species in this sample?
3. Using the Distributions widget, what is the most common TimeOfDay for sightings?
4. Which Region has the highest variability in animal Count (check using box plots)?
5. Plot a scatter plot of Count (x-axis) vs Region (as color). What pattern (if any) do you notice?

Dataset 2: Student Sleep Survey

Use the file student_sleep.csv. This dataset contains student-reported data on sleep and study habits.

6. Using Feature Statistics, what is the average GPA across all students?
7. What is the range of HoursSleep (min and max)?
8. What Major shows the highest GPA on average?
9. Create a scatter plot of HoursStudy vs GPA, colored by CaffeineIntake. What relationship do you observe?
10. Based on the Box Plot of GPA grouped by Major, which majors show the most GPA variability?

Lab 3

Normalizing Data

In data mining, differences in measurement scale (like inches and centermeters to measure length) across variables can distort results. This is especially when using methods based on distance or similarity of which in data mining there are many uses such as clustering where scale is critical or results will be distorted. For example, a variable ranging from 0 to 10,000 will dominate another ranging from 0 to 10, even if both are equally important.

To fix this, we normalize the data. There are several normalization techniques. This lab focuses on Z-score normalization, using the normal score system from the standard normal distribution. This is a standard method that adjusts each value based on its distance from the mean in terms of standard deviations. After transformation, all variables share a mean of 0 and a standard deviation of 1, making them directly comparable.

3.1 Lesson Steps

Step 1: Start a New Workflow and Load Data

Open Orange and start a new workflow. From the Data menu, drag a CSV File Import widget onto the canvas.

CSV File Import

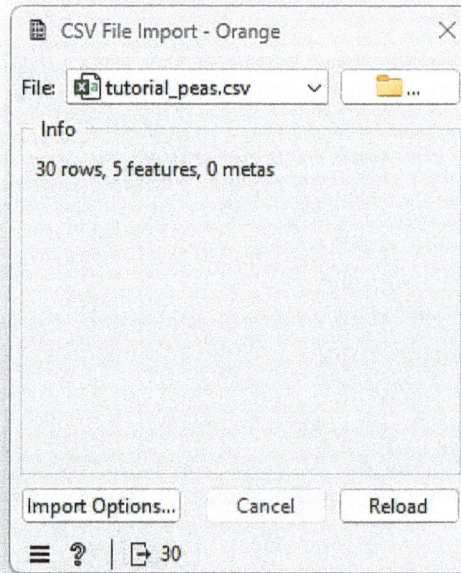

The CSV File Import widget allows you to bring raw data into Orange. This is the starting point for any data analysis or preprocessing task. Set the widget to import the file 'tutorial_peas.csv'.

Step 2: Set Data Types

Double-click the CSV File Import widget. Click Import Options and ensure that the numeric variables are correctly set to Numeric using the column type drop downs.

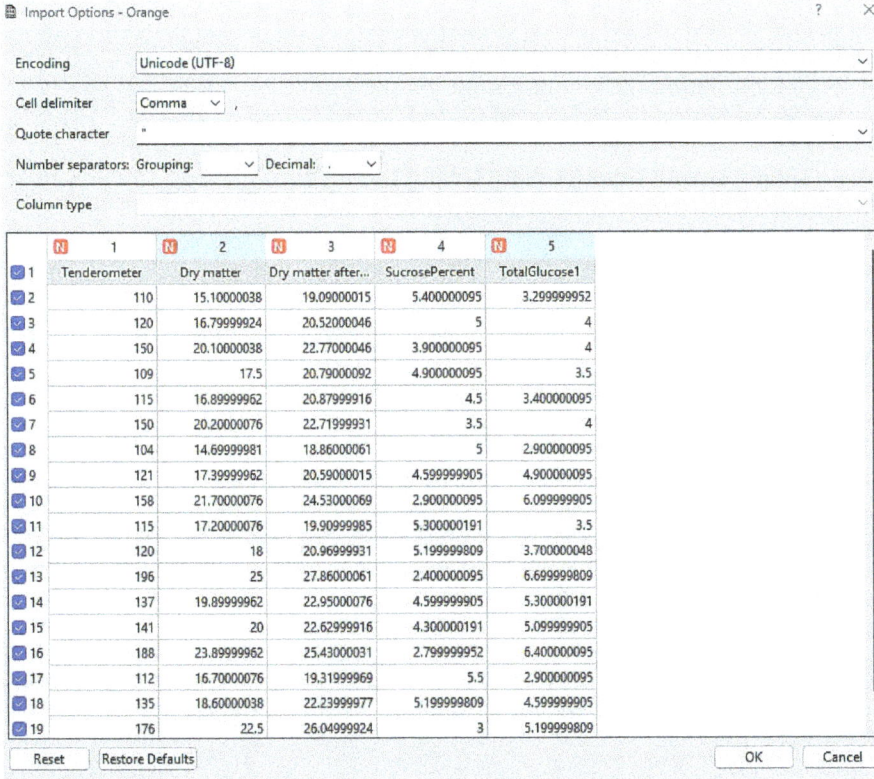

Orange may not detect imported data types correctly, so it's essential to confirm this manually.

Notice that in the original data the scales are all different. If we used this data as is the variable with the highest scale (Tenderometer in this case) would dominate analyses that are dependent on measurement scale and we don't want to do this. This is why we go through the preprocessing step of normalizing which puts all the data on the same scale so there is no impact of the original measurement scale.

Step 3: Add Preprocess Widget

From the Transform menu, add a Preprocess widget. Connect it to the CSV File Import widget.

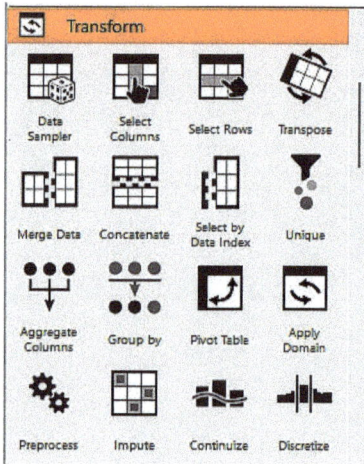

The Preprocess widget is used to apply data cleaning or transformation techniques like normalization, discretization, and imputation.

Step 4: Set Normalization Method

Double-click the Preprocess widget. Click and select Normalize Features from the list. Choose Standardize for the normalization method. Standardize converts values to standard normal (aka: z) scores so they have a mean of 0 and a standard deviation of 1. (Note remove any other listed operations on the right side, sometimes Orange puts in defaults).

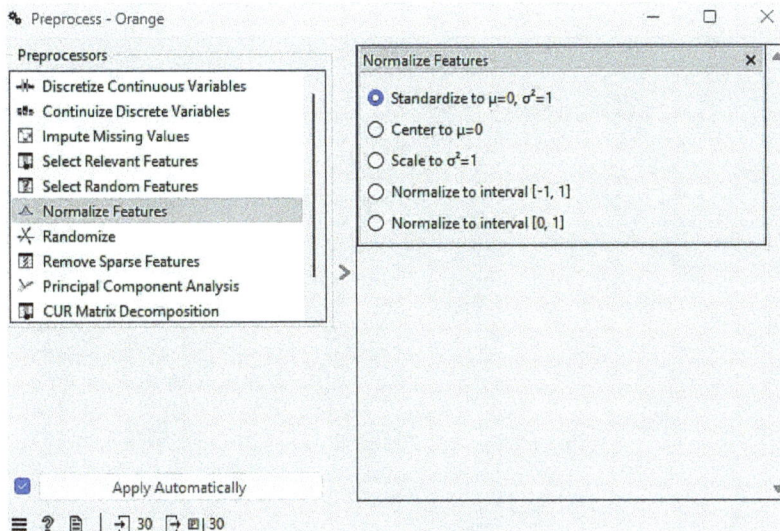

Step 5: View Normalized Data

From the Data menu, add a Data Table widget. Connect it to the output of the Preprocess widget. Note the connector (the line linking the widgets) should say "Preprocessed Data".

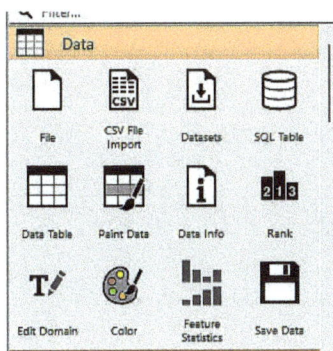

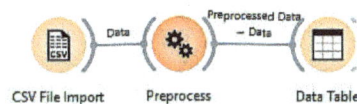

Double-click to open the Data Table.

		Tenderometer	Dry matter	matter after freez	SucrosePercent	TotalGlucose1
Data Table - Orange						
Info	1	-0.918	-1.46837	-1.30033	1.12985	-0.79108
30 instances (no missing data) 5 features	2	-0.583	-0.90018	-0.75149	0.75635	-0.25519
No target variable. No meta attributes.	3	0.420	0.20276	0.11207	-0.27079	-0.25519
	4	-0.951	-0.66623	-0.64786	0.66297	-0.63797
Variables	5	-0.750	-0.86676	-0.61332	0.28947	-0.71453
☑ Show variable labels (if present)	6	0.420	0.23619	0.09288	-0.64430	-0.25519
☐ Visualize numeric values	7	-1.118	-1.60206	-1.38861	0.75635	-1.09731
☑ Color by instance classes	8	-0.550	-0.69965	-0.72462	0.38284	0.43382
Selection	9	0.688	0.73753	0.78757	-1.20456	1.35250
☐ Select full rows	10	-0.750	-0.76649	-0.98561	1.03648	-0.63797
	11	-0.583	-0.49911	-0.57878	0.94310	-0.48486
>	12	1.959	1.84047	2.06564	-1.67144	1.81184
	13	-0.014	0.13592	0.18116	0.38284	0.74005
	14	0.119	0.16934	0.05834	0.10271	0.58693
	15	1.691	1.47283	1.13299	-1.29793	1.58217
	16	-0.851	-0.93361	-1.21206	1.22323	-1.09731
	17	-0.081	-0.29858	-0.09135	0.94310	0.20415
	18	1.290	1.00491	1.37095	-1.11118	0.66349
	19	-1.520	-1.43495	-1.43083	0.66297	-1.40354
	20	-0.316	0.23619	-0.06832	-0.27079	-0.25519
	21	0.956	0.87122	0.76454	-1.39131	0.96972
Restore Original Order	22	-0.717	-1.06730	-1.03934	0.75635	-1.70976
☑ Send Automatically	23	-0.048	0.20276	0.14278	0.10271	-0.71453

≡ ? 🖹 | ⇥ 30 ⇤ 30 | 30

This view shows your dataset after normalization. You'll see that the values have been rescaled, making them more suitable for analytics that depend on scale.

Step 6: Compare Original and Normalized Data

Add another Data Table widget and connect it directly to the original CSV File Import widget.

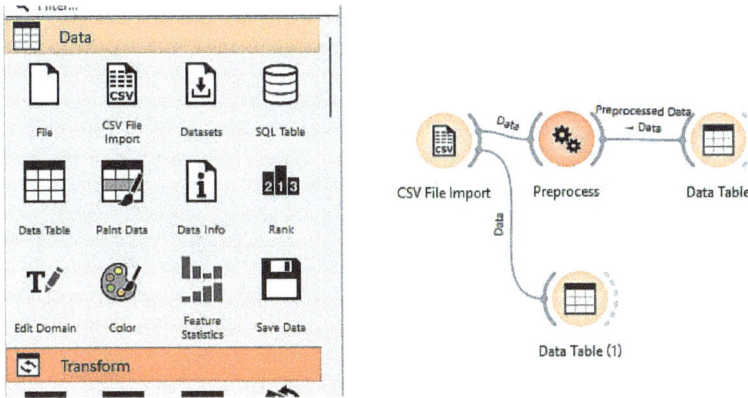

Open both tables to compare raw vs. normalized values.

	Tenderometer	Dry matter	natter after free	SucrosePercent	TotalGlucose1
1	-0.918	-1.46837	-1.30033	1.12985	-0.79108
2	-0.583	-0.90018	-0.75149	0.75635	-0.25519
3	0.420	0.20276	0.11207	-0.27079	-0.25519
4	-0.951	-0.66623	-0.64786	0.66297	-0.63797
5	-0.750	-0.86676	-0.61332	0.28947	-0.71453
6	0.420	0.23619	0.09288	-0.64430	-0.25519

Data Table - Orange

	Tenderometer	Dry matter	matter after freez	SucrosePercent	TotalGlucose1
1	110	15.1	19.09	5.4	3.3
2	120	16.8	20.52	5	4
3	150	20.1	22.77	3.9	4
4	109	17.5	20.79	4.9	3.5
5	115	16.9	20.88	4.5	3.4
6	150	20.2	22.72	3.5	4
7	104	14.7	18.86	5	2.9
8	121	17.4	20.59	4.6	4.9
9	158	21.7	24.53	2.9	6.1

Data Table (1) - Orange

This comparison helps you understand the effect of normalization. In data mining it is often very important to use normalized data.

3.2 Wrap-Up

This lab showed how Z-score normalization evens the playing field when variables are on different scales. By standardizing each feature to have a mean of zero and a standard deviation of one, we avoid skewed results in distance-based or variance-based analyses. With your data now on the same scale, when you do datamining wor you don't have to be worrying about one variable overpowering the others.

3.3   Exercises

Normalizing Data

1. Start a new workflow and load each dataset using the CSV File Import widget.
2. Add a Preprocess widget and apply Z-score normalization to all numeric features.
3. Use Data Table or other visualization widgets to compare original and normalized values.
4. Explore summary statistics (mean, standard deviation) before and after normalization.
5. Observe changes in data spread and variability across features.
6. Discuss why normalization is important for downstream analyses like clustering or PCA.

Dataset 1: Student Performance

Use the file student_scores.csv. This dataset contains student performance metrics on different scales—perfect for exploring normalization.

1. What are the mean and standard deviation of the Test_Score before normalization?
2. After Z-score normalization, what is the Z-score for a Test_Score of 95?
3. In the normalized data, which variable appears to have the most variability (widest spread)?
4. Compare the original and normalized values for Sleep_Hours. What differences do you notice?
5. What would happen if we performed further analysis on this data without normalizing?

Dataset 2: Nutrition Tracker

Use the file nutrition_data.csv. This data includes various dietary metrics on very different scales, which is ideal for normalization exercises.

6. What is the range of Calories before normalization?
7. After standardization, what is the Z-score for a Fiber_Grams value of 26?
8. Which feature has the smallest spread in Z-scores after normalization?
9. Using a Data Table widget, compare original vs normalized Fat_Intake. What pattern do you see?

Lab 4

Principal Components Analysis (PCA)

Principal Component Analysis (PCA) is a powerful mathematical method for simplifying complex datasets. Instead of analyzing many separate variables that may overlap in what they tell us, PCA helps us find a smaller number of new variables—called principal components—that capture the most important patterns in the data.

In this lab, we'll explore how PCA works step by step in Orange. By the end, you'll see how PCA transforms raw variables into clearer, more manageable dimensions that still reflect the structure of the original data.

4.1 Lesson Steps

Step 1: Load the Data

Start a New Workflow in Orange and place a CSV File Import widget from the Data menu into your workflow.

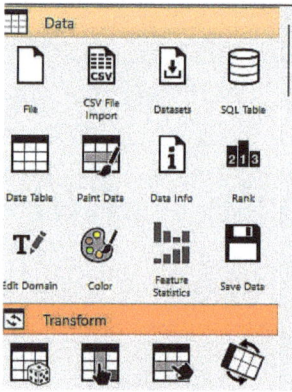

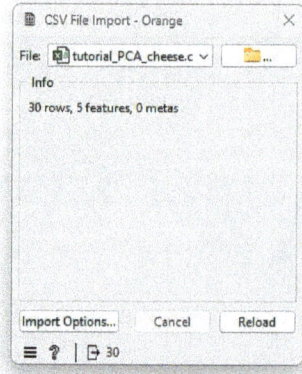

Double click the widget and follow steps to upload the CSV file named tutorial_PCA_cheese.csv using the import widget.

Step 2: Data Options

Because a CSV file is being uploaded it is a file type with no metadata. Therefore, we must tell it what types of data are in the columns. To do this double click the widget, click import options (bottom left) and change the column types by selecting each column and using the pull down. Case should be set to ignore and the other columns to numeric.

Import Options - Orange   ?   ✕

Encoding	Unicode (UTF-8)	⌄

Cell delimiter	Comma ⌄	,

Quote character	"	⌄

Number separators: Grouping:	⌄ Decimal: , ⌄

Column type	Numeric	⌄

	1	N 2	N 3	N 4	N 5
☑ 1	Case	Acetic	H2S	Lactic	Taste
☑ 2	1	4.543	3.135	0.86	12.3
☑ 3	2	5.159	5.043	1.53	20.9
☑ 4	3	5.366	5.438	1.57	39
☑ 5	4	5.759	7.496	1.81	47.9
☑ 6	5	4.663	3.807	0.99	5.6
☑ 7	6	5.697	7.601	1.09	25.9
☑ 8	7	5.892	8.726	1.29	37.3
☑ 9	8	6.078	7.966	1.78	21.9
☑ 10	9	4.898	3.85	1.29	18.1
☑ 11	10	5.242	4.174	1.58	21
☑ 12	11	5.74	6.142	1.68	34.9
☑ 13	12	6.446	7.908	1.9	57.2
☑ 14	13	4.477	2.996	1.06	0.7
☑ 15	14	5.236	4.942	1.3	25.9
☑ 16	15	6.151	6.752	1.52	54.9
☑ 17	16	6.365	9.588	1.74	40.9
☑ 18	17	4.787	3.912	1.16	15.9
☑ 19	18	5.412	4.7	1.49	6.4

Reset   Restore Defaults   OK   Cancel

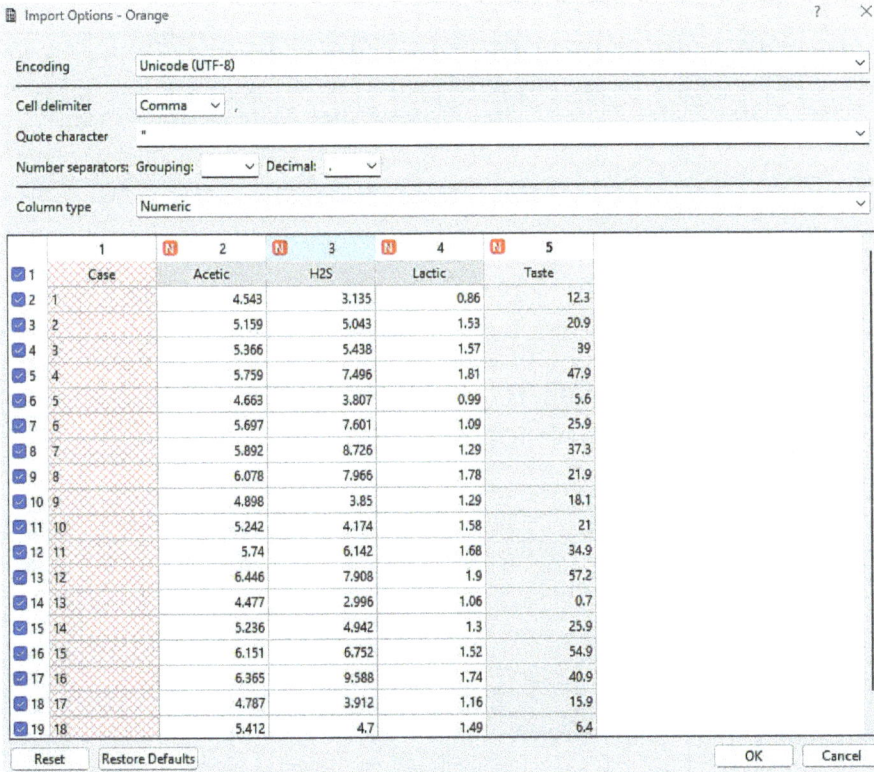

Step 3: Select Feature Columns

The numeric variables we are going to use for PCA are called features (input variables). We need to tell Orange what these columns are as this ensures we don't accidentally include irrelevant or non-numeric information (like IDs or labels) in the PCA (an alternative would be to create a subset dataset with only the numeric variables, but we will not do this here).

Add a Select Columns widget (under the Transform menu) and connect it to the CSV file import widget.

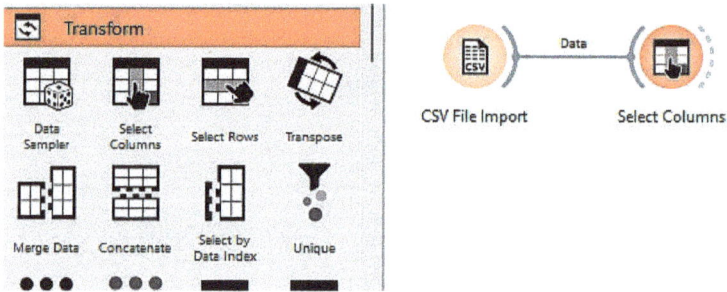

Open the Select Columns widget and select the four cheese attribute variables as features. In doing so we are explicitly choosing which variables we want to analyze with PCA.

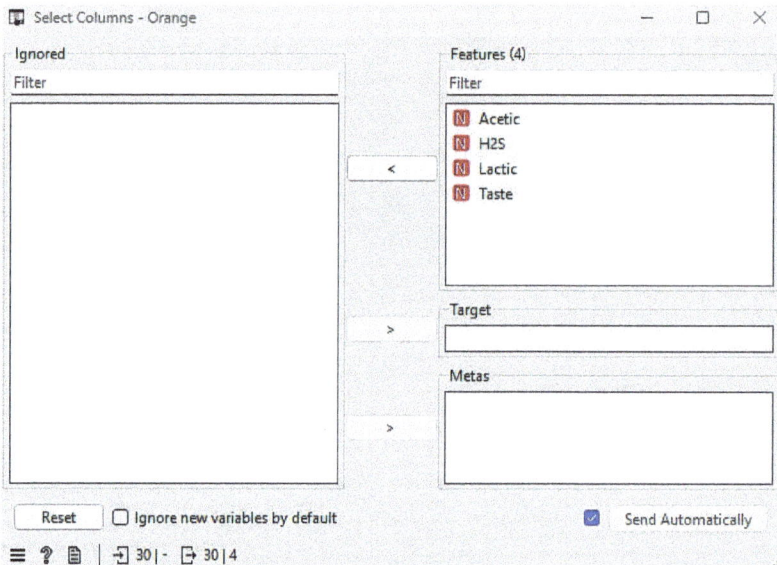

Step 4: Normalize the Variables

From the Transform section of widgets add a Preprocess widget and connect it to the Select Columns widget as shown.

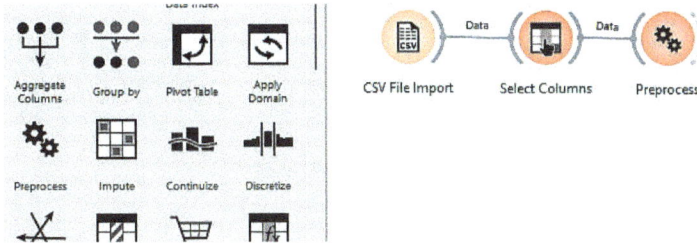

Open the Preprocess widget and set it to Normalize Features with standardize selected (mean = 0, SD = 1).

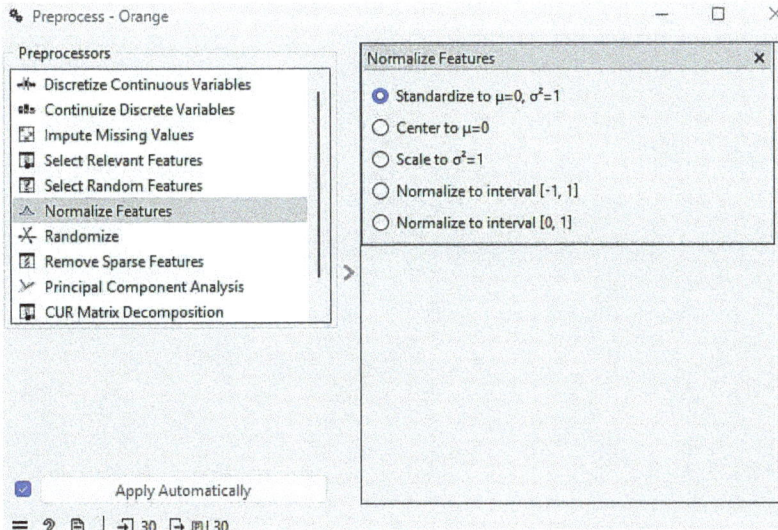

PCA is sensitive to the scale of variables. If one variable has larger numbers (e.g., fat content vs. flavor score), it could dominate the PCA. Standardization rescales each feature, so they all contribute equally, using z-scores.

Step 5: Check the Normalized Data

Add a Data table widget and connect it to the Preprocess widget. Make sure the connector says, "Preprocessed Data" (if not click on the connector - not the widgets - and fix).

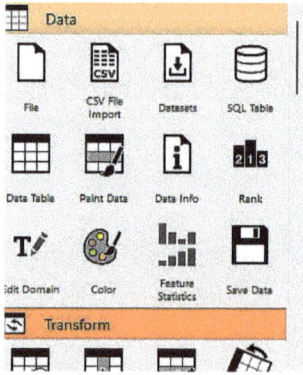

Open the table to make sure the data is normalized using standard normal scores (mean 0, SD 1).

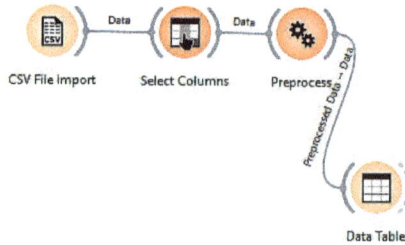

	Acetic	H2S	Lactic
1	-1.70152	-1.34222	-1.9535
2	-0.60403	-0.42980	0.2967
3	-0.23523	-0.24091	0.4310
4	0.46495	0.74325	1.2370
5	-1.48772	-1.02087	-1.5169
6	0.35449	0.79346	-1.1810
7	0.70190	1.33145	-0.5094
8	1.03329	0.96801	1.1363
9	-1.06904	-1.00030	-0.5094
10	-0.45616	-0.84536	0.4646
11	0.43110	0.09575	0.8004
12	1.68893	0.94027	1.5393
13	-1.81911	-1.40870	-1.2818
14	-0.46685	-0.47810	-0.4758
15	1.16335	0.38746	0.2631
16	1.54462	1.74367	1.0019
17	-1.26680	-0.97066	-0.9460
18	-0.15328	-0.59383	0.1623

Always inspect the data after transformation to confirm it worked as expected. The values should now be centered around zero and on the same scale. This is critical before running PCA for valid results.

Step 6: Apply PCA

Add a PCA widget (from the Unsupervised menu) and connect it to the Preprocess widget. Note do this on a separate branch from where the data table is connected as shown.

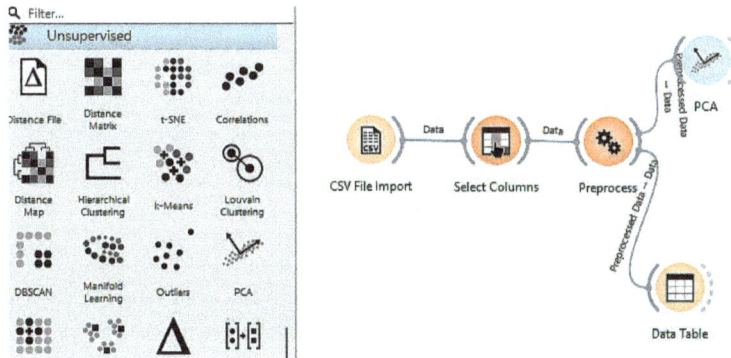

Open the PCA widget which will show the Scree plot. Since 85% of the variability is captured by 2 principal components 2 is a good choice here. Make sure components selection (upper left) is set to 2.

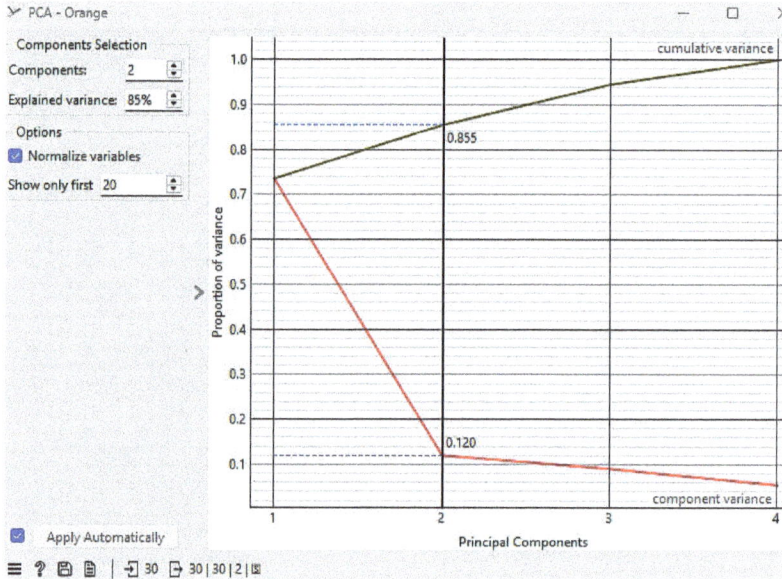

PCA transforms the original variables into principal components—new variables that are combinations of the originals. These components are uncorrelated and sorted by how much variation they capture. The scree plot helps you decide how many components to keep. In this case, two components capture most of the important information.

Step 7: Output Principal Components

Connect a data table widget to the PCA widget. Doing it this way appends the principal components which are the transformed variables to the normalized data table.

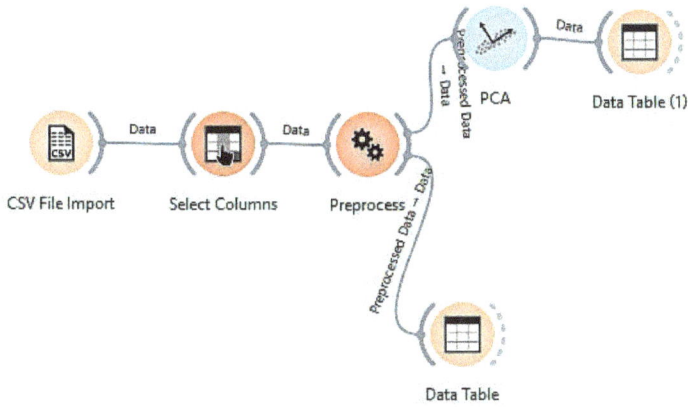

Open the table to see the results. You'll now see two new columns—these are the transformed variables, or principal components. They are combinations of the original variables but rotated and compressed in a way that preserves the structure in fewer dimensions. These can now be used in further analysis or visualizations.

Data Table (1) - Orange   —   □   ×

Info		PC1	PC2	Acetic	H2S
30 instances (no missing data)	variance	0.735363	0.119653		
4 features	1	-2.86007	-0.627133	-1.70152	-1.
No target variable.	2	-0.470934	-0.34678	-0.60403	-0.
2 meta attributes	3	0.448528	-0.622224	-0.23523	-0.
Variables	4	1.97352	-0.566906	0.46495	0.
☑ Show variable labels (if present)	5	-2.59117	-0.352425	-1.48772	-1.
☐ Visualize numeric values	6	0.024672	0.211696	0.35449	0.
☑ Color by instance classes	7	1.16833	-0.0042988	0.70190	1.
Selection	8	1.46652	0.653796	1.03329	0.
☐ Select full rows	9	-1.47677	-0.467286	-1.06904	-1.
	10	-0.528564	-0.155509	-0.45616	-0.
	11	0.986182	-0.0365258	0.43110	0.
	12	3.0968	0.129492	1.68893	0.
	13	-2.98511	-0.432245	-1.81911	-1.
	14	-0.659011	-0.295926	-0.46685	-0.
	15	1.85171	-0.0165728	1.16335	0.
Restore Original Order	16	2.64876	0.379249	1.54462	1.
☑ Send Automatically	17	-1.84386	-0.534885	-1.26680	-0.

≡ ? ▤ | ⇥ 30 ⇤ 30 | 30

Step 8: View Component Weights

Add another Data table widget and connect it to the PCA widgets second (bottom) output. Right-click the connection so it sends components not all data to the second data table (this is done by selecting the connector).

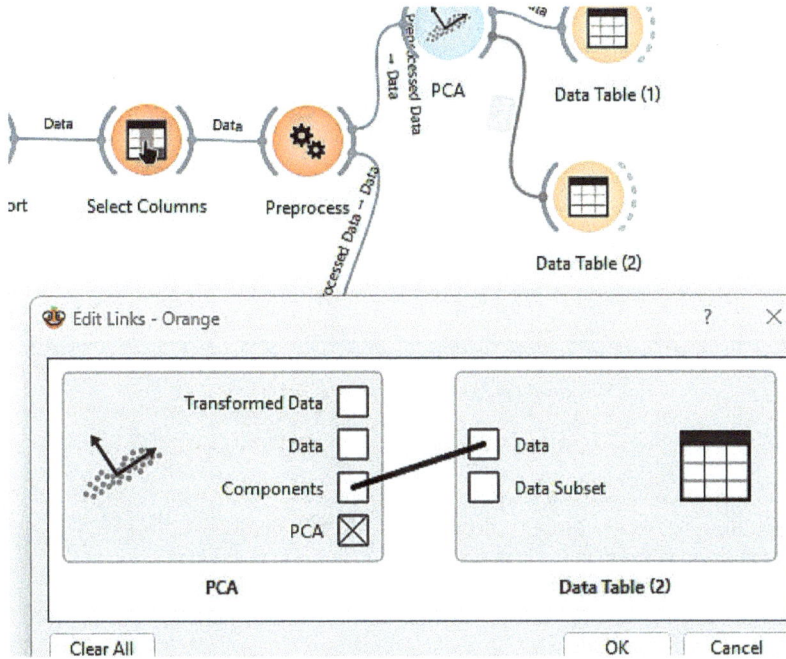

Each principal component is created by weighing the original features. These weights (or loadings) show how much each original variable contributes to each component. They're like the recipe for how to make the new variables from the old ones. Open the second data table to show the weights.

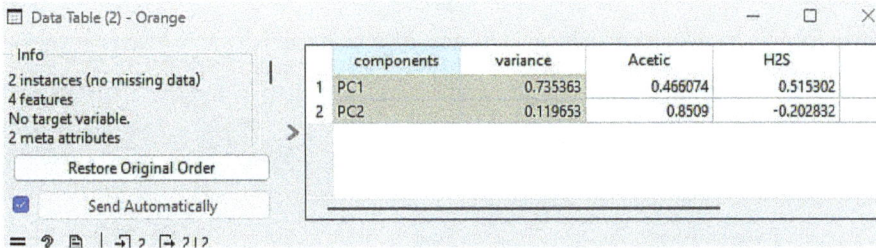

Step 9: Restructure the Component Table

The original component table can be hard to read—each row is a feature, and each column is a principal component. Add a Transpose widget from the Transform section and connect it to the component Data Table output. Add another Data Table to view the transposed version.

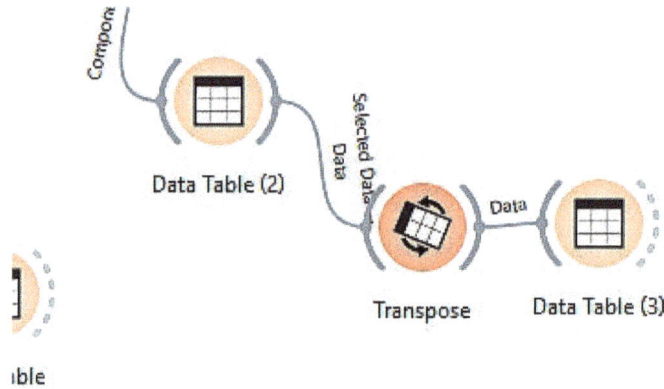

Transposing it makes it more readable: now each row is a component, and you can clearly see the weights across features. The % variance captured is also displayed under each PC, which helps in interpretation.

	Feature name	PC1 0.735363	PC2 0.119653
variance			
1	Acetic	0.466074	0.8509
2	H2S	0.515302	-0.202832
3	Lactic	0.502443	-0.0945225
4	Taste	0.514578	-0.475284

Info
4 instances (no missing data)
2 features
No target variable.
1 meta attribute

Variables
☑ Show variable labels (if present)
☐ Visualize numeric values

Restore Original Order

☑ Send Automatically

Step 10: Final Workflow

The final workflow should look something like this.

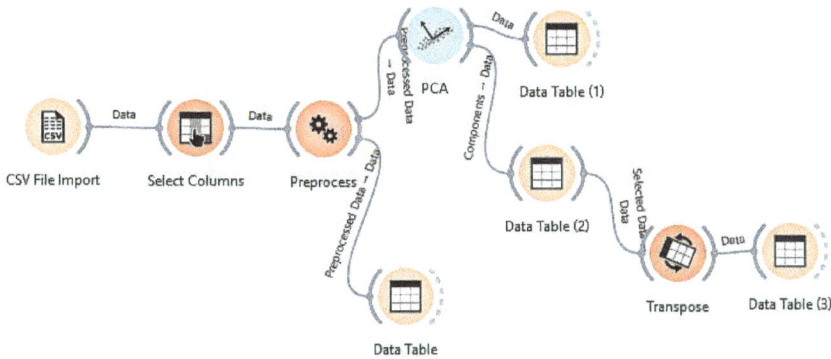

Step 11: Interpretation

When we perform Principal Component Analysis (PCA), we're trying to reduce a dataset with many variables down to a smaller number of new variables that still capture the most important information. These new variables are called principal components, and the first one, PC1, represents the direction of the strongest variation in the data. Rather than just looking at the raw variables like Acetic acid, H2S, Lactic acid, and Taste, PCA creates new combinations of them that better summarize patterns across all observations.

To understand how PC1 is constructed, we look at its loadings (see step 8). Loadings are simply the weights that tell us how much each original variable contributes to the principal component. For PC1 in this case, the loadings are around 0.466 for Acetic, 0.515 for H2S, 0.502 for Lactic, and 0.515 for Taste. This tells us that PC1 is a combination of all four variables, with each one playing an equal role (as the values are all around 0.5). These weights show us that PC1 is essentially measuring an overall "intensity" across all the variables — higher values in any of these tend to increase the PC1 score.

Once we know the loadings, we can calculate the scores. A score tells us how each observation (each row in our dataset) fits into this new dimension. But to calculate scores properly, we first standardize the data. After standardization, we multiply each standardized value by its corresponding loading and add them all up to get the score for that component.

For example, suppose the first row of our data has standardized values of −1.31 for Acetic, −1.25 for H2S, −1.03 for Lactic, and −0.84 for Taste. Using the PC1 loadings, we calculate:

$$PC1 = (-1.31 \times 0.466) + (-1.25 \times 0.515) + (-1.03 \times 0.502) + (-0.84 \times 0.515)$$

$$PC1 = -2.81$$

This score tells us that the first observation lies well below average on the PC1 axis. Since PC1 reflects overall levels of the four original variables, a negative score means this sample has relatively low values in those measurements, compared to the rest of the dataset.

To condense this into one summary. PC1 is a new variable that captures the main pattern in the data. The loadings tell us what original variables are responsible for this pattern, and the scores tell us how each individual case aligns with it. A high score means the observation has high values in the key contributing variables, while a low score indicates the opposite. This relationship — between components, loadings, and scores — is the core idea behind PCA, and it helps us simplify complex data into interpretable trends. If you have for example a dataset of 200 variables you could use PCA to reduce the dimensionality of the data to a smaller number of transformed variables which is very handy for interpretable analysis.

4.2 Wrap-Up

This lab walked through the process of applying Principal Component Analysis (PCA). Starting from raw data, we selected relevant features, standardized them, and used PCA to reduce dimensionality. Using principal components to reduce data dimensionality creates a simplified, structured view of the data that highlights its key patterns, making it easier to explore, visualize, or model in future steps.

4.3   Exercises

Principal Components Analysis (PCA)

1. Start a new workflow and load your dataset using the CSV File Import widget.
2. Confirm numeric data types for all features to be included in PCA.
3. Add a Preprocess widget and standardize the data to ensure all variables contribute equally.
4. Add a PCA widget and run it on the standardized data.
5. Examine the Scree plot to determine how many components explain most of the variance.
6. Review component loadings (weights) to understand which original features contribute most to each principal component.
7. Use PCA scatter plots or data tables to explore grouping or clustering patterns.
8. Repeat for any additional datasets provided.
9. Answer lab questions by interpreting variance explained, component weights, and PCA visualizations.

Dataset 1: Car Performance Metrics

Use the file car_specs.csv. This dataset contains vehicle performance attributes with different scales, making it ideal for PCA.

1. After standardizing the data, which feature shows the highest variability across the dataset?
2. According to the Scree plot in the PCA widget, how many components explain at least 85% of the variance?
3. Using the component table, which original variable contributes the most to the first principal component (PC1)?
4. What does a car with a negative PC1 score likely indicate about its performance?
5. Based on the PCA scatter plot, are there any clusters or groupings among the vehicles?

Dataset 2: Environmental Quality Indicators

Use the file environmental_quality.csv. This dataset includes regional environmental scores that benefit from dimensionality reduction.

6. Which two original variables contribute most strongly to PC1?

7. What percentage of total variance is explained by the first two principal components?

8. Which region has the highest score on PC2, and what does that suggest about its environment?

9. After transposing the component weight table, what feature shows the largest loading for PC2?

10. Describe in your own words how PCA could help policymakers understand environmental trends from this data.

Lab 5

Understanding Distance

Distance is a fundamental concept in machine learning and data analysis, particularly for clustering algorithms. However, distance calculations can be misleading if features are measured on different scales. This lab explores how normalization transforms raw data into data that produces meaningful distance measurements.

5.1 Lesson Steps

Step 1: Start Workflow and Load Data

Open Orange and start a new workflow. From the Data menu, drag a CSV File Import widget to the canvas. Load the file tutorial_Kmeans_salary.csv. This file contains the dataset we'll be using to explore distance metrics and normalization. Starting with the raw data gives a baseline to compare against the normalized version later.

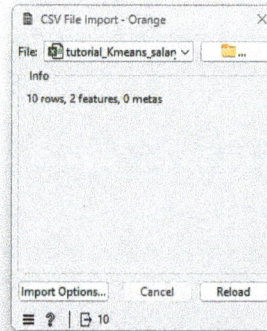

Step 2: Set Data Types

Double-click the CSV File Import widget. Click Import Options and set both columns to Numeric using the dropdown menus. Orange does not auto-detect data types. Distance calculations require numeric inputs, so setting both variables correctly ensures the model processes them properly.

Import Options - Orange   ?   ×

Encoding	Unicode (UTF-8)	⌄

Cell delimiter	Comma ⌄	,

Quote character	"	⌄

Number separators: Grouping: ⌄   Decimal: , ⌄

Column type	Numeric	⌄

	N 1	**N** 2
☑ 1	Age	Salary
☑ 2	20	40
☑ 3	23	50
☑ 4	24	45
☑ 5	23	50
☑ 6	40	81
☑ 7	43	85
☑ 8	42	87
☑ 9	35	82
☑ 10	70	30
☑ 11	68	37

Reset	Restore Defaults		OK	Cancel

Step 3: Connect to Distance Widget

From the Unsupervised menu, add the Distances widget to the canvas. Connect it to the CSV File Import widget. This widget calculates pairwise distances between instances in your dataset. It's important for many tasks in data mining.

Step 4: Select Distance Metric

Double-click on the Distances widget. For different data types (numeric, categorical, text), Orange automatically selects appropriate distance measures, but you can customize them using the Distance widget. Different options like Euclidean, Manhattan, or Cosine (for numeric/text) and Hamming (for categorical) are available. Choose Euclidean as the distance metric (NOT Euclidean(normalized)). Euclidean distance is the most used metric in data analysis. It literally is the disance formula (when two varaibles only are involved) used in high school geometry to determine the shortest distance between two points. It extends to n-dimensions and measures the shortest distance between points in multidimensional space.

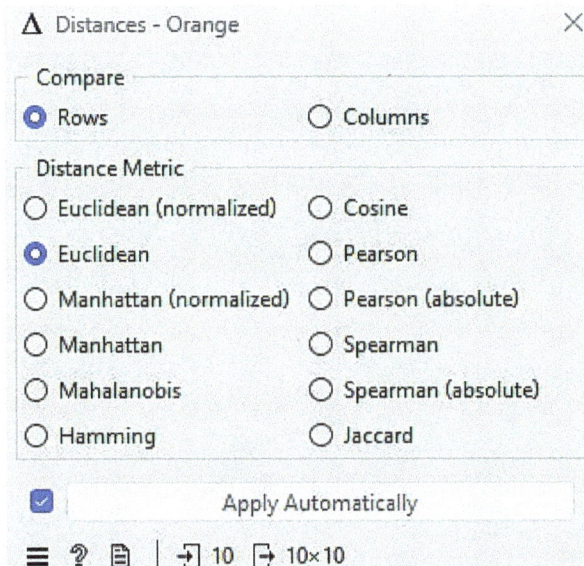

Step 5: View Distance Matrix

From the Unsupervised menu, add a Distance Matrix widget. Connect it to
the output of the Distances widget.

Open the Distance matrix. This displays the computed distances in a tabu-
lar format. It's useful to understand how similar or different data points are
before applying further processing.

Distance Matrix - Orange

	1	2	3	4	5	6	7	8	9	10
1		10.440	6.403	10.440	45.618	50.537	51.894	44.598	50.990	48.094
2	10.440		5.099	0.000	35.355	40.311	41.593	34.176	51.078	46.840
3	6.403	5.099		5.099	39.395	44.283	45.695	38.601	48.384	44.721
4	10.440	0.000	5.099		35.355	40.311	41.593	34.176	51.078	46.840
5	45.618	35.355	39.395	35.355		5.000	6.325	5.099	59.169	52.154
6	50.537	40.311	44.283	40.311	5.000		2.236	8.544	61.270	54.120
7	51.894	41.593	45.695	41.593	6.325	2.236		8.602	63.506	56.356
8	44.598	34.176	38.601	34.176	5.099	8.544	8.602		62.682	55.803
9	50.990	51.078	48.384	51.078	59.169	61.270	63.506	62.682		7.280
10	48.094	46.840	44.721	46.840	52.154	54.120	56.356	55.803	7.280	

Note however this distance matrix is on data that are not normalized. When using distance-based methods like k-NN or clustering in data mining on unnormalized values such as age and salary, features with larger numerical ranges (e.g., salary) can dominate the distance calculation. This skews the results by giving disproportionate influence on those features, potentially leading to misleading or biased groupings or predictions. Therefore, we don't want to use this distance data in analysis.

Step 6: Normalize the Data

Normalization scales all features to the same range, which is essential when variables have different units or scales. This ensures fair distance comparisons. Let's normalize the data.

From the Transform menu, add a Preprocess widget. Connect it to the CSV File Import widget.

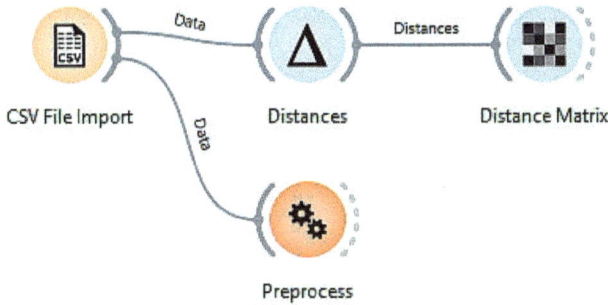

Double-click the Preprocess widget. Set it to Normalize features and select Standardize. Standardizing centers the data (mean = 0) and scales it (std dev = 1). This is a common method that ensures the influence of each feature is balanced during distance calculations.

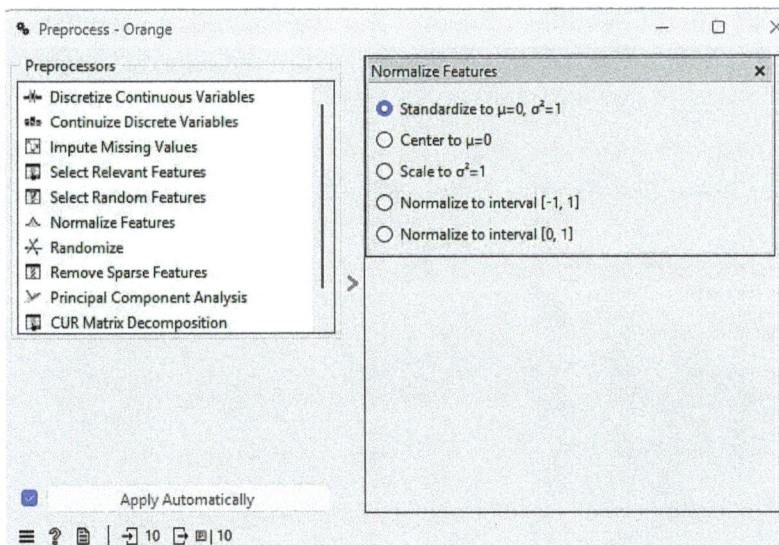

Step 7: View Normalized Data

Connect a Data Table widget to the Preprocess widget.

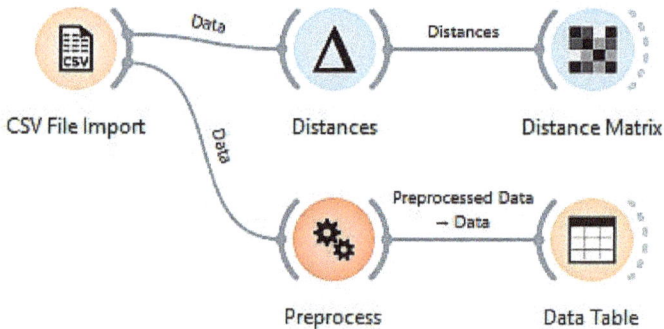

Double-click the Data Table to inspect the normalized values. Verifying the transformed data helps confirm that normalization was successful. You'll see that the values are now centered and scaled.

Step 8: Compute Distances on Normalized Data

Add a new Distances widget and connect it to the Preprocess widget. Then, connect it to a new Distance Matrix widget. By recalculating distances on normalized data, new distance metrics are not dependent on measurement scales used in the unscaled data (inches, dollars, etc.). This is critical in models sensitive to feature scale.

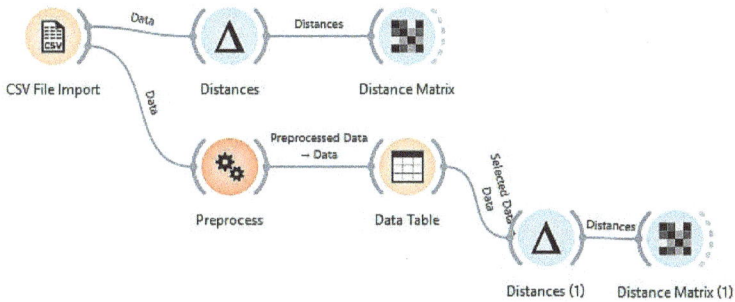

Step 9: View Normalized Distance Matrix

Double-click the new Distance Matrix widget to view results. This matrix shows the updated distances based on the standardized dataset.

	1	2	3	4	5	6	7	8	9	10
1		0.355	0.234	0.355	1.594	1.772	1.808	1.528	2.088	1.981
2	0.355		0.171	0.000	1.247	1.427	1.459	1.174	2.049	1.905
3	0.234	0.171		0.171	1.367	1.544	1.582	1.312	1.961	1.833
4	0.355	0.000	0.171		1.247	1.427	1.459	1.174	2.049	1.905
5	1.594	1.247	1.367	1.247		0.182	0.216	0.209	2.100	1.864
6	1.772	1.427	1.544	1.427	0.182		0.078	0.345	2.142	1.901
7	1.808	1.459	1.582	1.459	0.216	0.078		0.333	2.220	1.979
8	1.528	1.174	1.312	1.174	0.209	0.345	0.333		2.253	2.023
9	2.088	2.049	1.961	2.049	2.100	2.142	2.220	2.253		0.247
10	1.981	1.905	1.833	1.905	1.864	1.901	1.979	2.023	0.247	

Labels: Enumerate   ☑ Send Automatically

Step 10: Compare Results

Comparing the original and normalized distance matrix reveals how normalization impacts distance relationships.

Raw data may contain scale biases (e.g., salary measured in thousands vs. age). Normalizing removes this imbalance, providing more reliable distance calculations for modeling tasks.

5.2 Wrap-Up

Working through this lab, you've seen firsthand how raw data can distort distance measurements when features are on different scales. By normalizing the data, you made those comparisons fair—ensuring that one variable doesn't overpower another just because of its units. Normalization and distance computation is essential groundwork for accurate clustering and other distance-based methods. Comparing both matrices side-by-side, it's clear: normalization isn't just a technical detail—it's what makes distance meaningful.

5.3 Exercises

Understanding Distance

1. Start a new workflow and load your dataset using the CSV File Import widget.
2. Confirm numeric data types for all features used in distance calculations.
3. Add a Distance widget to calculate the distance matrix using raw data.
4. Add a Preprocess widget and apply normalization or standardization to features.
5. Recalculate the distance matrix using the normalized data.
6. Compare distance matrices before and after normalization to understand the impact on distances.
7. Use the Data Table widget to inspect distances between specific pairs of instances.

Dataset 1: Salary and Age

Use the file employee_data.csv. This dataset includes Age and Salary — two features with very different scales.

1. Before normalization, which variable dominates the distance metric — Age or Salary? Why?
2. After normalization, how does the Distance Matrix change for two employees with similar ages but different salaries?
3. What is the distance between Employee E003 and E009 in the unnormalized Distance Matrix?
4. What is the same distance after normalization? How does it compare?
5. Why is normalization critical?

Dataset 2: Health Metrics

Use the file health_data.csv. This dataset includes Body Mass Index (BMI) and Daily Steps — again, with values on very different scales.

6. Before normalization, which feature (BMI or DailySteps) contributes more to Euclidean distances? Explain.
7. After applying standardization, how does the Distance Matrix change between P001 and P015?
8. Compare a pair of individuals with similar BMI but very different step counts — what happens to their distance after normalization?

9. In your own words, why is standardization often preferred over min-max normalization in distance-based models?

10. Based on the normalized Distance Matrix, which two individuals are most similar? Support your answer with matrix values.

Lab 6

Hierarchical Clustering

Clustering helps us find structure in data when we don't have predefined labels (categorical data) that we can group it by. Often data may be novel and we don't know what the labels or patterns are. There are different methods of clustering, although all are based on distances using normalized data and operate by finding data values that are mathematically close (clustering).

Hierarchical clustering works by building a tree of nested clusters that lets us explore relationships at different levels.Ot agglomerates data together as it clusters resulting in a unified tree with branches. Steps to perform hierarchical clustering include loading and preparing measurement data, calculating distances, and building dendrograms using different linkage methods.

6.1   Lesson Steps

Step 1: Start Workflow and Load Data

Open Orange and begin a new workflow. From the Data menu, add a CSV File Import widget to the canvas.

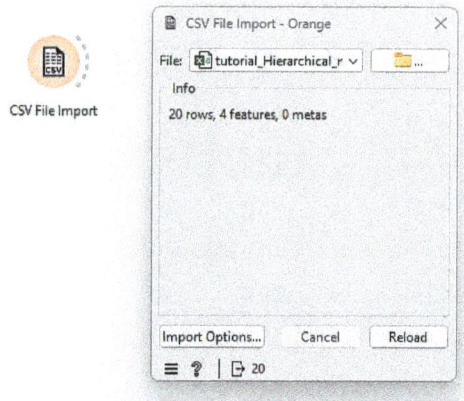

Load the dataset tutorial_Hierarchical_measurements.csv. This dataset contains measurement data that will be used for hierarchical clustering. Importing it is the first step to building your clustering model.

Step 2: Set Data Types

Double-click the CSV File Import widget. Click Import Options and set all variables to Numeric using the column type drop down.

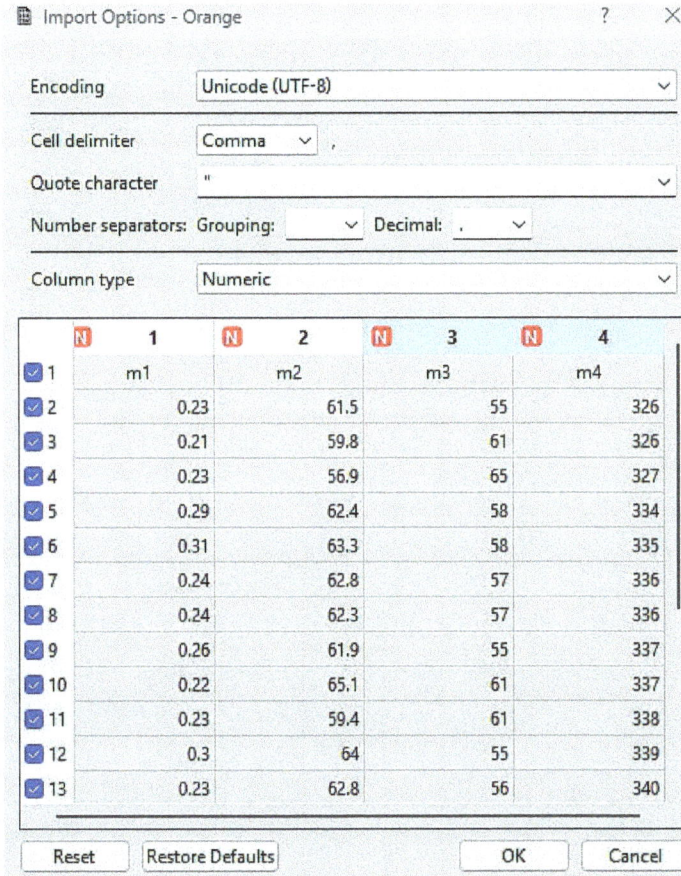

Hierarchical clustering requires numerical input to compute distances. Ensuring the variables are numeric allows proper distance calculation between data points (distances are only computed on numeric variable type).

Step 3: Normalize the Data

From the Transform menu, add a Preprocess widget. Connect it to the CSV File Import widget.

Double-click the Preprocess widget and select Normalize Features > Standardize.

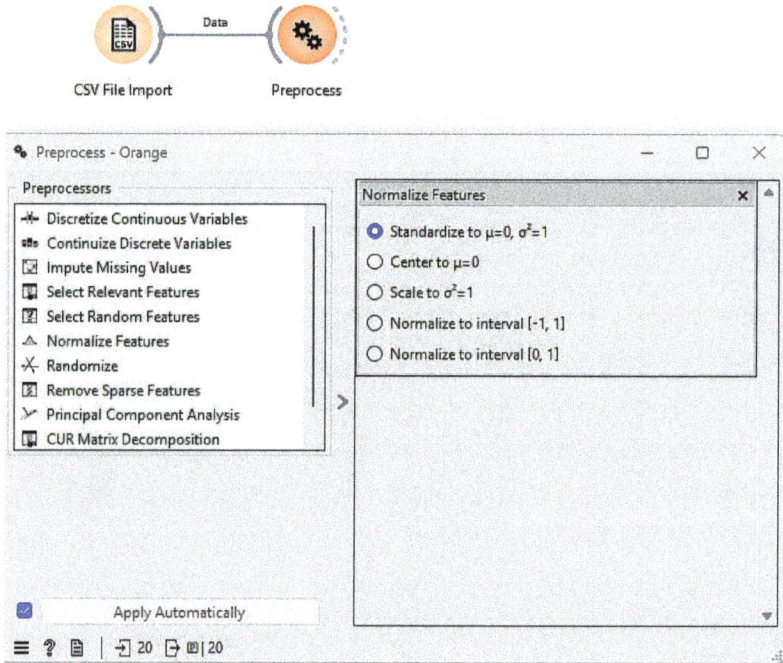

Normalization standardizes the data (mean = 0, std. dev = 1), which prevents variables with larger scales from dominating the distance computation.

Step 4: Check Normalized Data

Add a Data Table widget from the Data menu. Connect it to the Preprocess widget.

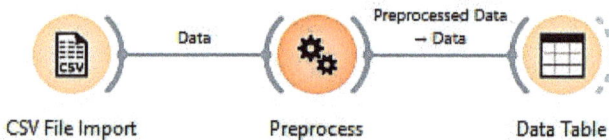

Double-click the Data Table widget to view the normalized values.

Viewing the normalized data ensures that preprocessing was applied correctly. You should see centered and scaled values for each feature.

Step 5: Compute Distances

From the Unsupervised menu, add a Distances widget. Connect it to the Preprocess widget. Double-click and set the Distance Metric to Euclidean.

This widget calculates pairwise distances between data points. Euclidean distance is the most used metric for clustering on data that is numeric and since this data is all numeric this is the distance computation we will use here.

Step 6: View Distance Matrix

Add a Distance Matrix widget from the Unsupervised menu. Connect it to the Distances widget. Open the distance matrix.

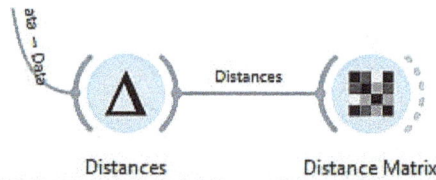

	1	2	3	4	5	6	7	8	9	10
1		2.231	4.127	2.149	2.726	1.646	1.548	1.643	3.139	2.764
2	2.231		2.120	2.861	3.525	2.586	2.422	2.975	3.240	1.665
3	4.127	2.120		4.173	4.760	4.321	4.122	4.523	4.848	2.377
4	2.149	2.861	4.173		0.718	1.353	1.336	1.331	2.537	2.496
5	2.726	3.525	4.760	0.718		1.830	1.890	1.795	2.684	3.124
6	1.646	2.586	4.321	1.353	1.830		0.273	0.972	1.888	2.300
7	1.548	2.422	4.122	1.336	1.890	0.273		0.866	2.079	2.086
8	1.643	2.975	4.523	1.331	1.795	0.972	0.866		2.817	2.513
9	3.139	3.240	4.848	2.537	2.684	1.888	2.079	2.817		3.123
10	2.764	1.665	2.377	2.496	3.124	2.300	2.086	2.513	3.123	

Labels: Enumerate   Send Automatically

The matrix shows how far each data point is from each other. The distance matrix is a foundation component of hierarchical clustering as it is the basis data used for the clustering.

Step 7: Run Hierarchical Clustering

Add a Hierarchical Clustering widget from the Unsupervised menu. Connect the Distances widget to the Hierarchical Clustering widget.

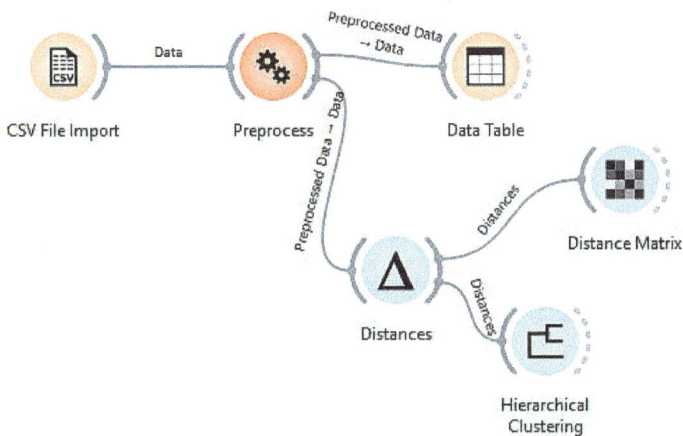

This widget builds a hierarchical tree (dendrogram) based on the pairwise distances, revealing nested clusters in the data.

Step 8: View the Dendrogram

Double-click the Hierarchical Clustering widget. You'll see a tree diagram (dendrogram) showing how clusters form by merging smaller groups. By default, Orange uses single linkage (min distance between clusters). Linkage is a metric that computes distances bewteen clusters (distance itself is between data points) and there are different linkage methods.

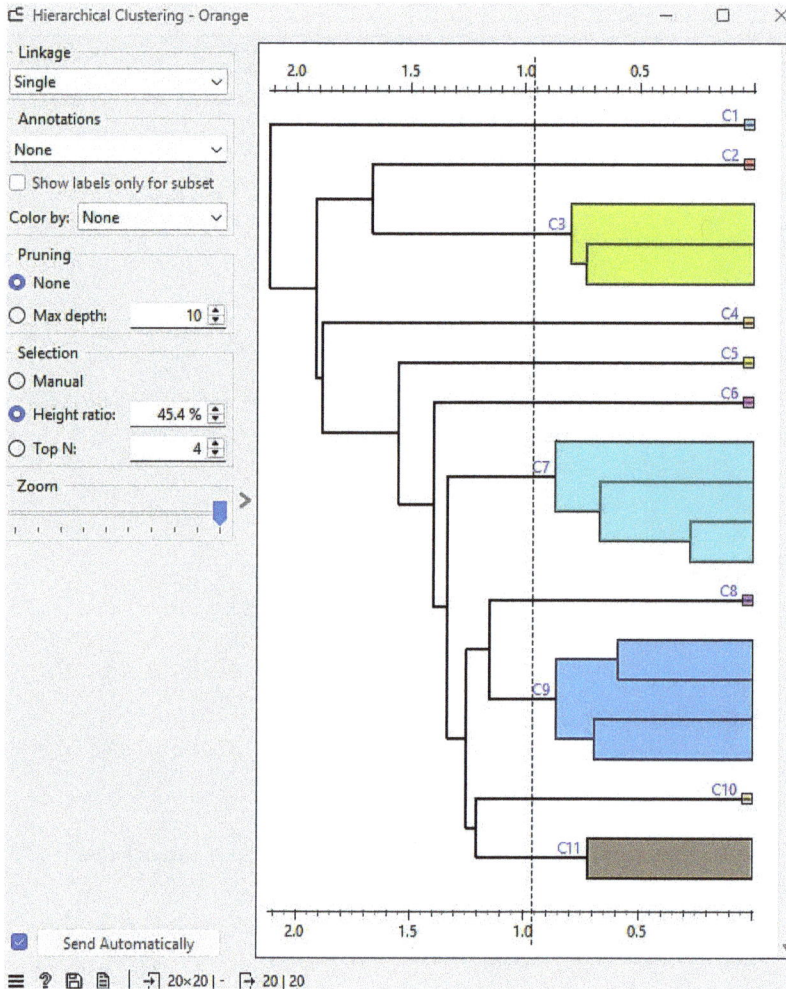

Step 9: Explore Linkage Methods

Change the linkage setting within the Hierarchical Clustering widget to Ward linkage. Then look at the dendrogram again. This dendrogram is much easier to interpret clusters.

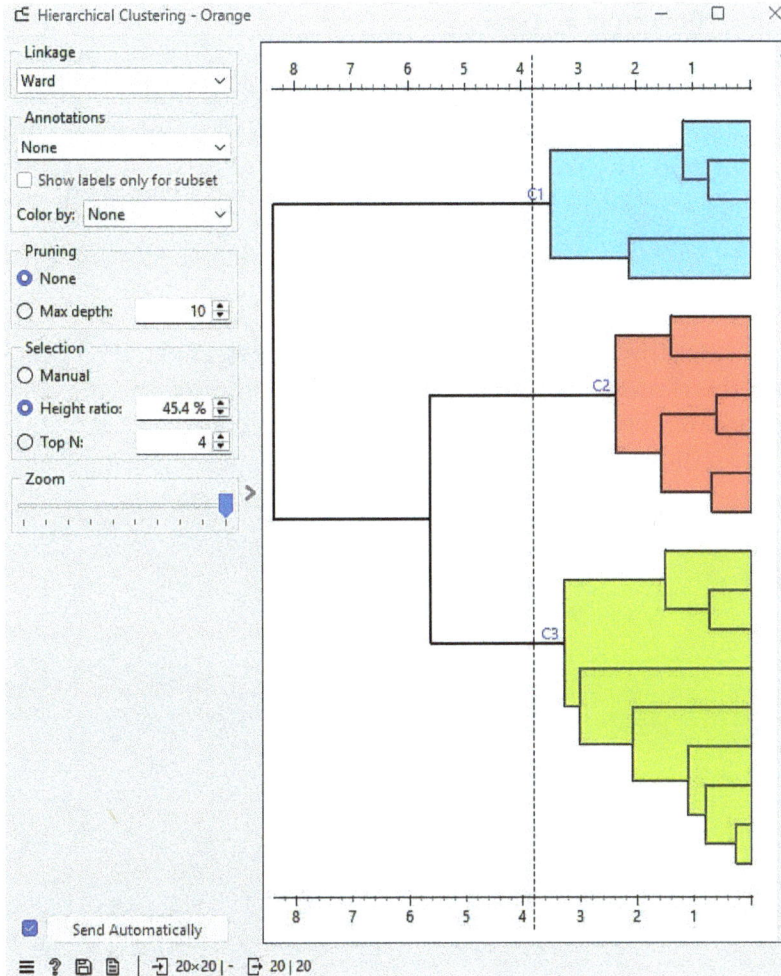

Different linkage methods change how clusters are merged. Ward linkage tends to create more balanced clusters. Try different methods to see how they affect the clustering outcome.

Step 10: Interpret Clustering

Experiment with different linkage methods and examine the dendrogram structure. You can cut the dendrogram at different levels to form flat clusters.

Hierarchical clustering is exploratory. The goal is to take unfamiliar data and look at patterns that may define groups and structure to the data. There may not be a "right" answer. Cluster results interpretation often depends on domain expertise (aka: someone familiar with the contextual meaning of data being clustered).

6.2 Wrap-Up

This lab worked through the key steps in hierarchical clustering—from pre-processing the data to building and exploring a dendrogram. This type of clustering is a flexible way to uncover structure in complex data. As you saw, your interpretation depends on both the linkage method and how you slice the tree. There's no one-size-fits-all answer to cluster results.

6.3 Exercises

Hierarchical Clustering

1. Start a new workflow and load your dataset using the CSV File Import widget.
2. Verify that features are numeric and properly formatted for clustering.
3. Add a Preprocess widget and normalize or standardize your data for distance calculations.
4. Use the Distance widget to compute the distance matrix (e.g., Euclidean distance).
5. Add a Hierarchical Clustering widget and connect it to the distance matrix.
6. Experiment with different linkage methods (single, complete, Ward) to observe cluster structure changes.
7. Open the Dendrogram widget to visualize clusters and cut the tree to identify major groupings.
8. Compare cluster results across linkage methods and interpret based on domain knowledge.

Dataset 1: Seed Nutritional Composition

Use the file seed_composition.csv. It contains basic nutrient data for different seed types.

1. After standardizing, which variable had the largest spread (based on values in the normalized table)?
2. In the Euclidean distance matrix, which two seeds were closest in distance?
3. With default (single linkage), how many major clusters appear in the dendrogram?
4. After switching to Ward linkage, how does the dendrogram structure change?
5. What kind of food product might the cluster containing Chia and Flax represent (based on features)?

Dataset 2: City Climate Patterns

Use the file city_climate.csv, which contains average annual climate values from different cities.

6. What is the normalized distance between Phoenix and Las Vegas? How

similar are they?

7. Which two cities are most distant according to the Euclidean distance matrix?

8. After clustering with Ward linkage, identify two clear geographic-based clusters. What traits unify them?

9. How does the clustering change when you switch to complete linkage?

10. Based on the dendrogram, where does Anchorage cluster and why might that make sense?

Lab 7

K Means Clustering

Clustering is one of the core tools used in unsupervised learning, and K-Means is one of the simplest and widely used clustering methods. K-Means clustering is an algorithm that groups data into K distinct clusters based on similarity (as measured by smallest distance between points). It works by assigning each data point to the nearest cluster center (centroid) and then updating the centroids based on the average of the assigned points. This process repeats until the cluster centers stop changing significantly.

In this lab,we will walk through the full process: preparing and normalizing the data, running the K-Means algorithm, and evaluating the quality of your clusters using silhouette scores. You will be able to interpret the clustering results both visually and numerically.

_____

7.1 Lesson Steps

Step 1: Start Workflow and Load Data

Open Orange and start a new workflow. From the Data menu, add a CSV File Import widget. Load the file: tutorial_Kmeans_salary.csv.

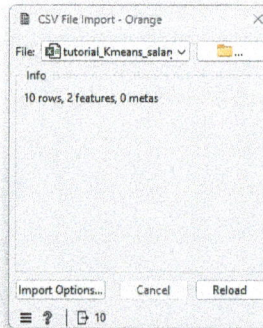

This dataset includes variables salary and age which will be used to cluster observations. K-Means groups have similar data points based on distance between them.

Step 2: Set Data Types

Double-click the CSV File Import widget. Click Import Options and set both columns to Numeric using the column type dropdown. When CSV files are loaded Orange doesn't necessarily know their data type so be sure to set data types correctly.

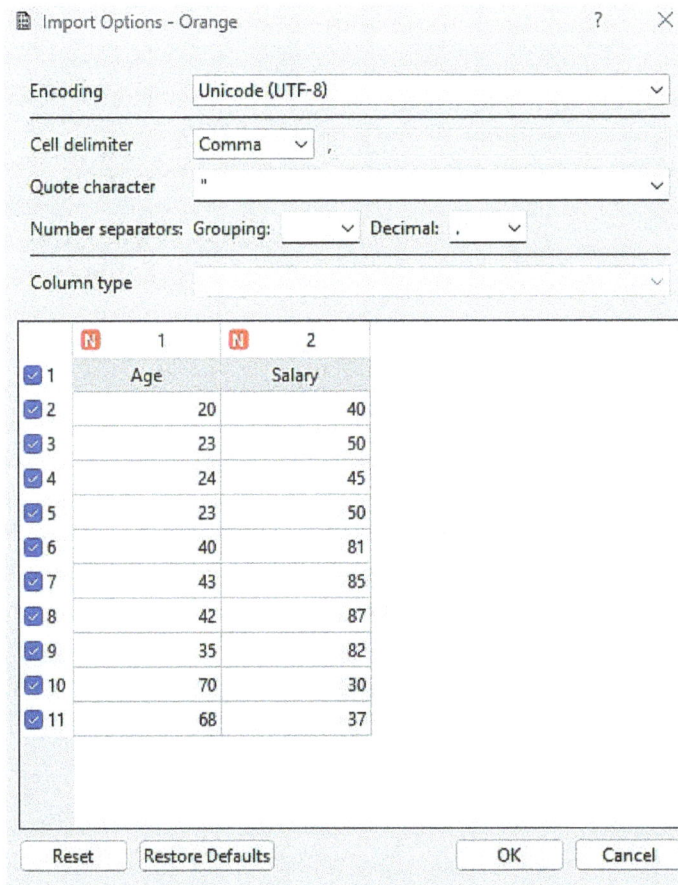

K-Means relies on numerical input for distance calculations. If variables are not set to numeric, the model will not work properly.

Step 3: Normalize the Data

From the Transform menu, add a Preprocess widget. Connect it to the CSV File Import widget. Double-click the Preprocess widget and select Normalize Features > Standardize.

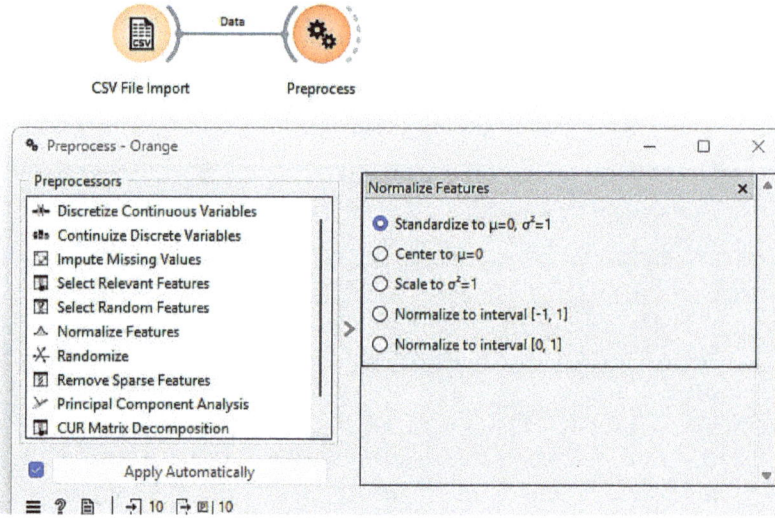

Standardizing ensures that all variables contribute equally to the clustering process, especially when they're measured on different scales (e.g., dollars vs. square footage).

Step 4: Check the Normalized Data

Add a Data Table widget. Connect it to the Preprocess widget. Open the table to inspect the normalized values.

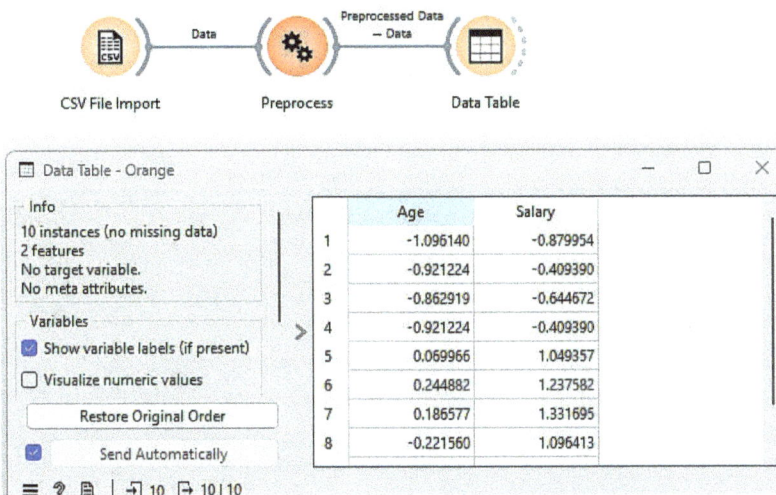

This step confirms that your data has been correctly transformed. Values should now be centered around 0 with standard deviation of 1.

Step 5: Setup K Means

From the Unsupervised menu, add a K-Means widget. Connect it to the Preprocess widget. Double-click the K-Means widget to view silhouette score analysis (note to do this you must choose 'From' and a range under Number of clusters)

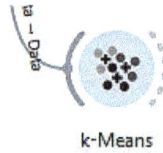

k-Means

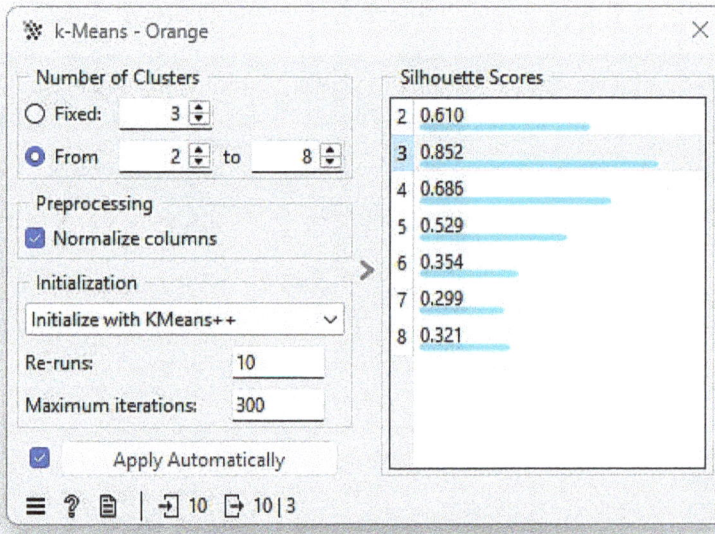

The silhouette score evaluates how well each point fits into its cluster. A higher score suggests better-defined clusters. Use this to decide the optimal number of clusters.

Step 6: Run K-Means

Set Number of Clusters to Fixed = 3 in the K-Means widget settings since this is the highest score and appears to be the optimal number of clusters.

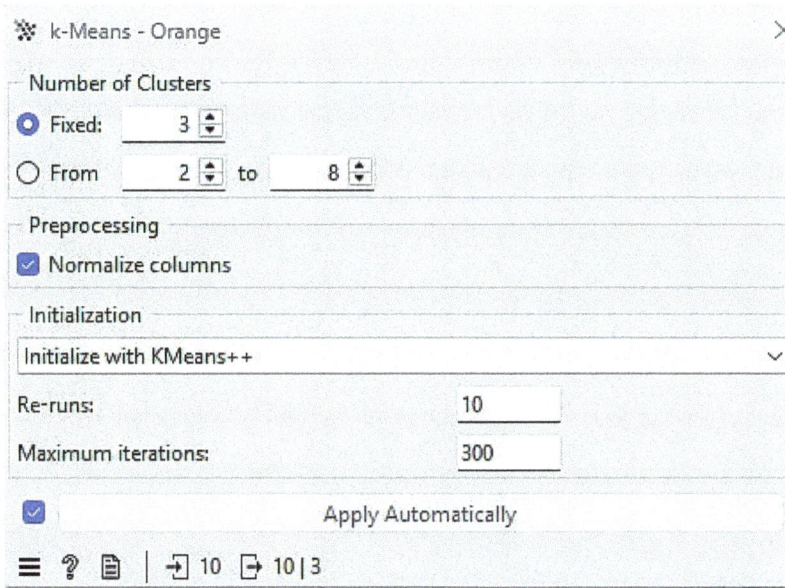

The analysis shows that k = 3 gives the best silhouette score. Setting k to 3 will group your data into three distinct clusters.

Step 7: Visualize the Clusters

From the Visualize menu, add a Scatter Plot widget. Connect it to the K-Means widget.

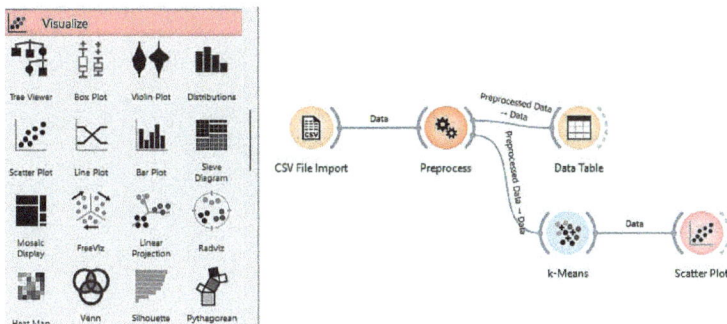

Open the scatter plot and in the scatter plot settings, set Color and Label to Cluster.

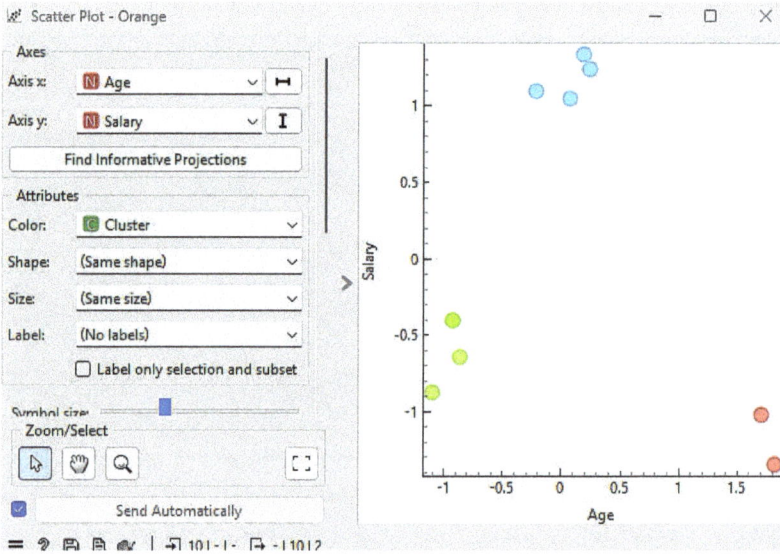

This shows the clustering result visually. You can easily see how data points were grouped and whether there's clear separation between clusters.

Step 8: Output Cluster Data

Add two Data Table widgets to the K-Means widget. Connect (so it just says 'Data' on the connector) one to the Annotated Data output of the K-Means widget. Connect the other to the Centroids output (changed on the connector by clicking on the connector and mapping the data).

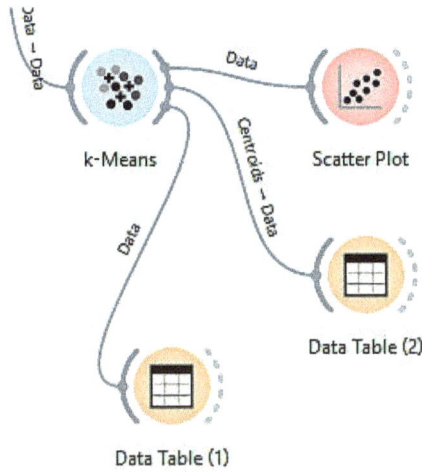

Annotated Data includes the original dataset with cluster assignments and silhouette scores.

		Cluster	Silhouette	Age	Salary
1	C3		0.717124	-1.096140	-0.879954
2	C3		0.727501	-0.921224	-0.409390
3	C3		0.727451	-0.862919	-0.644672
4	C3		0.727501	-0.921224	-0.409390
5	C1		0.724575	0.069966	1.049357
6	C1		0.727792	0.244882	1.237582
7	C1		0.727435	0.186577	1.331695
8	C1		0.709303	-0.221560	1.096413
9	C2		0.729474	1.819126	-1.350517

Centroid Data provides the final center of each cluster on a normalized scale, along with average silhouette scores for those clusters.

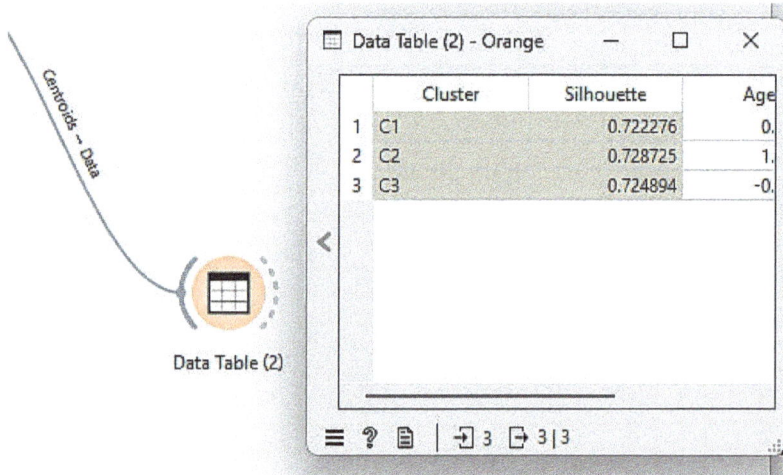

Data Table (2)

If you have different output in the data tables, be sure to select the correct output (Annotated or Centroids) by clicking the connection line and choosing the desired output.

7.2 Wrap-Up

This lab walked you through applying K-Means clustering. You prepared the data, ran the clustering algorithm, and used silhouette scores to judge how well the clustering performed. K-Means is straightforward to implement but requires thoughtful setup—especially when choosing the number of clusters and making sure your data is on the right scale.

7.3   Exercises

K-Means Clustering

1. Start a new workflow and load your dataset using the CSV File Import widget.
2. Check that all features used for clustering are numeric and properly formatted.
3. Add a Preprocess widget and normalize the features (e.g., Standardize) to ensure fair clustering.
4. Add a K-Means widget; set the number of clusters (k) as desired (commonly start with 2 or 3).
5. Connect the normalized data to the K-Means widget and run clustering.
6. Add an Evaluation widget like Silhouette Plot to assess cluster quality.
7. Use a Scatter Plot widget (or other visualization) to view clusters and centroids visually.
8. Optionally, adjust the number of clusters (k) and observe changes in silhouette scores and cluster separation.

Dataset 1: Tech Salaries

Use the file tech_salaries.csv. It contains fictional tech employee data with age and salary columns.

1. What does the silhouette score tell you about the quality of clustering with k = 3?
2. Which age and salary ranges appear in the same cluster after K-Means with k = 3?
3. How do the centroids relate to the original dataset variables (Age and Salary)?
4. In your scatter plot, how well-separated are the clusters visually?
5. How would increasing k to 5 affect silhouette scores and interpretability?

Dataset 2: City Rent and Commute

Use the file city_living.csv. It includes monthly rent and average commute time per city.

6. After normalization, which variable (Rent or Commute) had more influence on clustering—why?
7. What silhouette score do you get with k = 2, and how does it compare

to k = 3?

8. Which cities fall into the high-cost, long-commute cluster when k = 3?

9. Based on centroid values, what defines the lowest-cost cluster?

10. In your visualization, are there any overlapping clusters? What might that suggest about rent and commute relationships?

Lab 8

Logistic Regression

Logistic regression is a classification algorithm used when the dependent variable is binary (two categories). Although binary may sound limiting keep in mind everything can be made binary if restructured into 'this' (outcome of focus) and 'not this' (everything else) regardless of how many outcomes there are.

This lab will teach you how to setup, run and interpret a basic logistic regression classification algorithm. It is perhaps the simplest and most understandable classification algorithm used in data mining.

8.1 Lesson Steps

Step 1: Load Data

Start a new workflow in Orange. Add a CSV File Import widget from the Data menu. Upload the file named tutorial_logReg_adult.csv.

CSV File Import

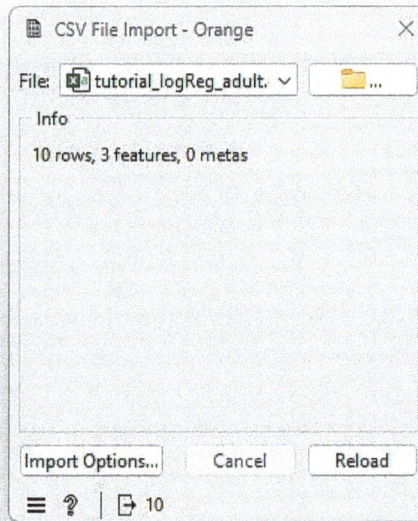

Loading the dataset is the first step in building your logistic regression model. Orange works best with standard file types like CSV (vs proprietary file types such as SPSS). This dataset includes a binary target variable needed for classification.

Step 2: Set Import Options

Double click to open the CSV file import widget to show the import options window. Ensure the variable Adult_Binary is set as a categorical (not numeric) variable. For logistic regression to work properly, the dependent variable must be binary categorical (values like 0/1, yes/no). Setting it as numeric would result in incorrect model behavior.

Step 3: Add Select Columns Widget

From the Transform menu, drag a Select Columns widget to the canvas. This widget allows you to choose which columns to use in the model. You define your features (independent variables) and your target (dependent variable) here.

Connect it to the CSV File Import widget.

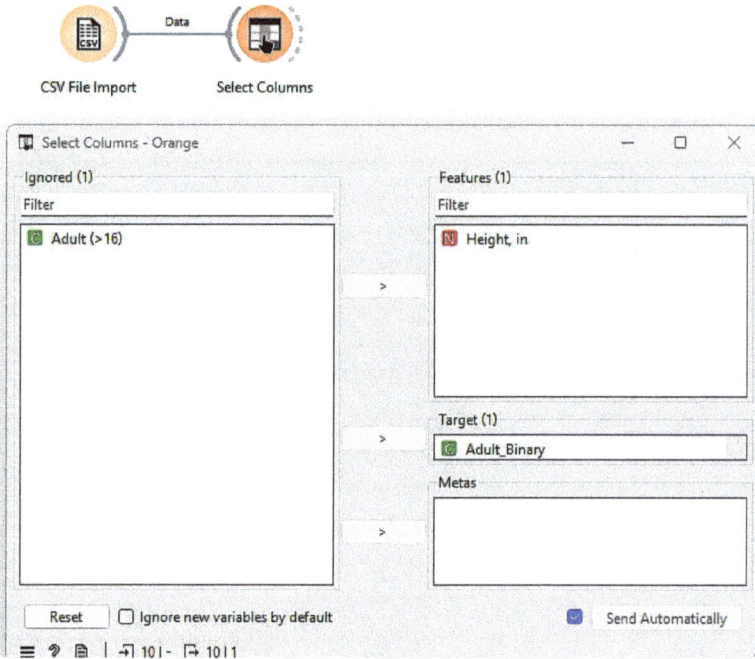

Step 4: Set Model Options

Double-click the Select Columns widget. Assign the correct target variable
and choose which features to include. Set any unused variables to ignored.
Classification models must always have a correct target variable assigned (this
is a common error issue when running such algorithms in Orange if this is not
correctly set).

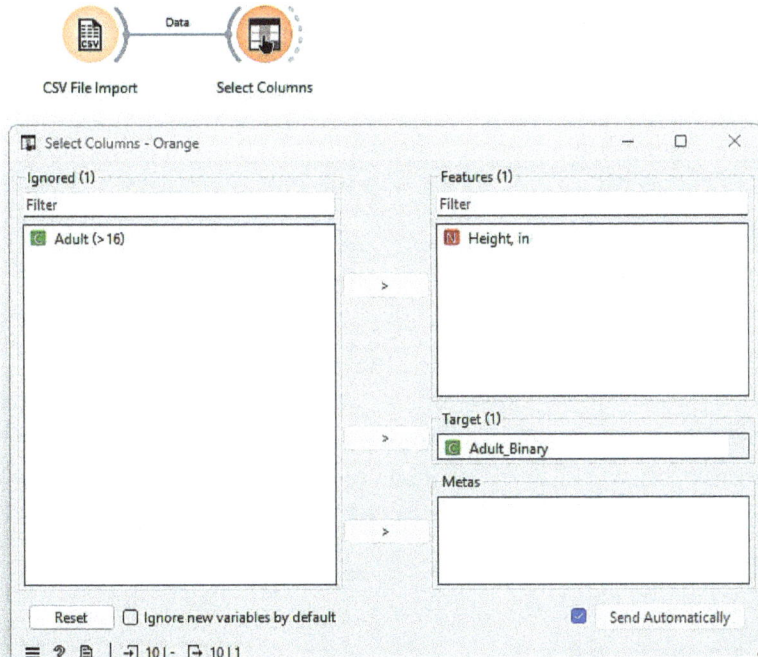

In regression tasks, it's crucial to clarify which variables are being predicted (target) and which are predictors (features). Ignoring irrelevant columns avoids unnecessary noise in the model.

Step 5: Box Plot Visualization

From the Visualize menu, add a Box Plot widget. Connect it to the output of the Select Columns widget.

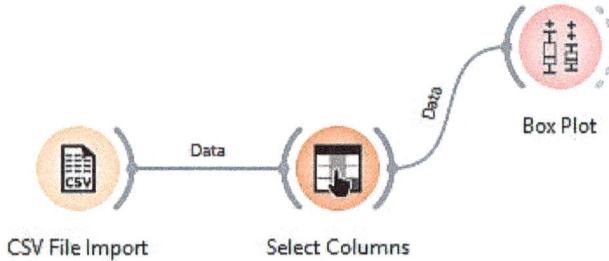

Box plots help visualize the spread of data and differences between groups. This is useful in checking if your target categories are distinct and suitable for logistic regression. Set the box plot to view height by adult binary.

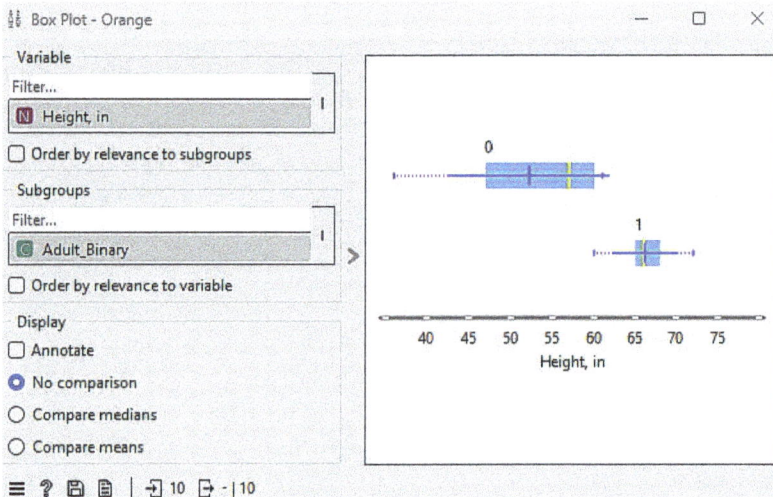

\stephead{Step 6: Set Up the Logistic Regression Model

From the Model menu, add a Logistic Regression widget. Connect it to the Select Columns widget. Double-click to open settings and set Regularization type to Ridge.

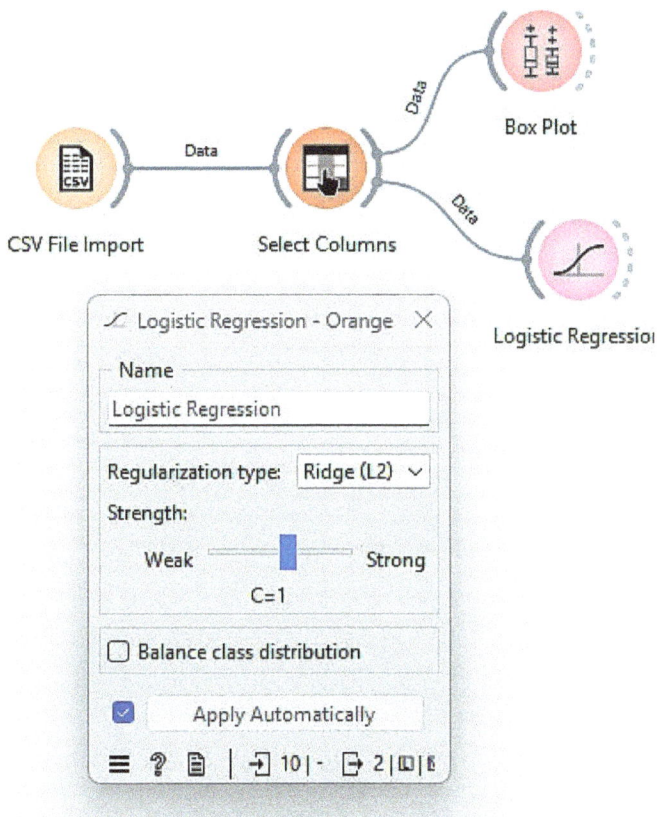

The logistic regression widget performs binary classification. Ridge regularization helps prevent overfitting by penalizing large coefficient values.

Step 7: Add Predictions Widget

Continue setting up the model workflow by adding a Predictions widget from under the Evaluate menu. Connect it to both the Logistic Regression widget and the data path.

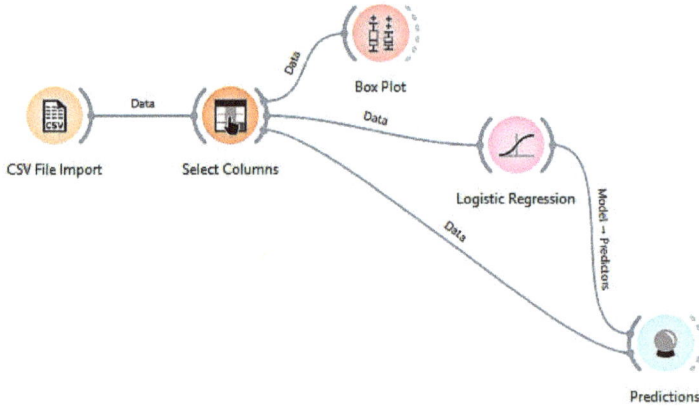

The Predictions widget shows how well your model is performing by comparing predicted vs actual outcomes. It is a key step in model validation.

Step 8: View Prediction Results

Double-click on the Predictions widget to display the results. Left side shows predicted values, right side shows original data.

This interface allows you to visually compare predictions to actual values. Misclassifications can be spotted easily here. In this model there is one misclassification (row 1 in the data) - you can see this because the prediction is 0 but the actual adult binary status is 1 (adult yes).

On the bottom is a matric 'CA' standing for classification accuracy. This is the overall percentage correct the model predicted (9/10 or 90% in this case) and is a straightforward way to evaluate model performance.

Step 9: Add Confusion Matrix

The confusion matrix provides a breakdown of true positives, true negatives, false positives, and false negatives. It's a standard tool for evaluating classification model performance and show accuracy of results.

Add a Confusion Matrix widget from the Evaluate menu. Connect it to the Predictions widget.

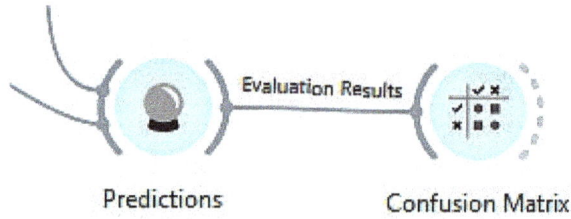

Step 10: View the Confusion Matrix

Double-click on the Confusion Matrix widget. This matrix is a visual display of classification accuracy and error rates, helping you assess model reliability. There is one misclassification in this result.

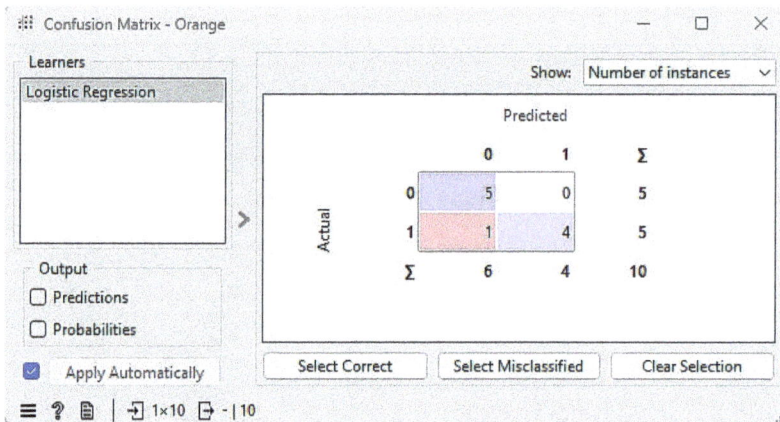

Step 11: Get Model Coefficients

Add a Data Table widget and connect it to the Logistic Regression widget. Make sure to configure the link (click on the connection line) and set the output to Coefficients.

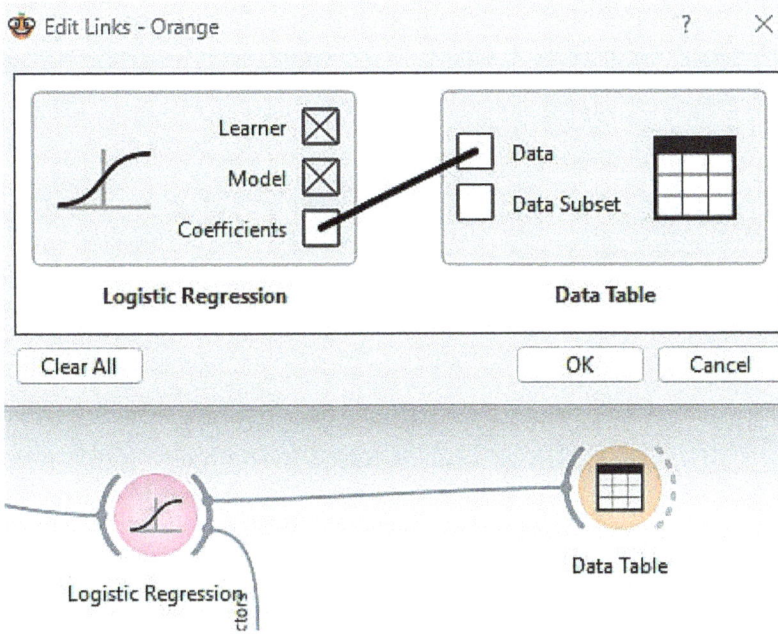

While Orange doesn't focus on statistical reporting, you can still retrieve the coefficients, which indicate how each feature affects the prediction. These can also be used to write and use the equation for the model.

Step 12: View Model Coefficients

Click on the Data Table widget connected to the Logistic Regression model.

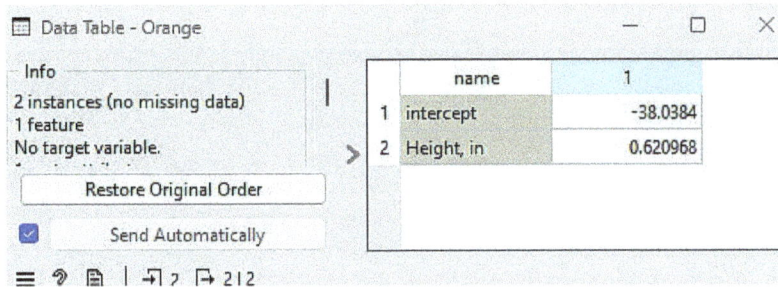

This shows the model coefficients used in predictions, which are actual numerical weights assigned to each feature in the model, offering insight into their influence.

8.2 Wrap-Up

In this lab, you built and evaluated a logistic regression model using Orange. You loaded a dataset, set up your target and features, and used box plots to explore how variables relate to class membership. You then trained a logistic regression model with ridge regularization and examined its predictions and accuracy. The confusion matrix helped you break down where the model got things right or wrong, while the coefficients offered insight into how different features contributed to the final prediction. This process mirrors the steps used in real-world classification tasks—giving you a hands-on understanding of how logistic regression works in practice.

8.3 Exercises

Logistic Regression

1. Start a new workflow and load your first CSV dataset using the CSV File Import widget.
2. Check and set data types correctly: ensure the target (dependent) variable is categorical binary, and features are numeric or categorical as appropriate.
3. Add a Select Columns widget to specify the features (independent variables) and the target variable. Ignore irrelevant columns.
4. Use visualization widgets like Box Plot to explore how features differ across target classes.
5. Add a Logistic Regression widget to build the classification model; set regularization parameters if desired (e.g., Ridge).
6. Add a Predictions widget and connect it to both the Logistic Regression model and the dataset to generate predicted labels.
7. Add a Confusion Matrix widget connected to the Predictions widget to evaluate model accuracy and errors.
8. Add a Data Table widget connected to the Logistic Regression widget (with output set to Coefficients) to examine feature influence.

Dataset 1: Adult Status Classification

Use the file adult_status.csv. It includes fictional data on age, education years, and income level to predict whether someone is considered an "Adult" (based on certain social thresholds).

1. Which variable (Age, Education_Yrs, or Income_K) has the most distinct separation in the box plot when grouped by Adult_Binary?
2. What accuracy does your model achieve using the confusion matrix?
3. Which class (0 or 1) has more false positives in the prediction?
4. How does ridge regularization help your model in this case?
5. Which feature has the strongest coefficient in the model output?

Dataset 2: Health Behavior Prediction

Use the file health_check.csv. It includes health behavior data to predict whether someone is likely to be at risk (Risk_Binary = 1).

6. According to your box plot, which variable best separates risky vs. non-risky individuals?

7. What is the model's confusion matrix output, and how many total mis-classifications are present?
8. Are smokers always classified as high-risk? Support with evidence from the prediction table.
9. How would the model change if Hours_Exercise was ignored in the Select Columns widget?
10. What would be a useful application for this model in a real-world health setting?

Lab 9

Decision Trees

Decision trees are a simple yet powerful tool for classification. They work by taking the entire dataset and then splitting data into branches based on feature values, creating a model that's easy to understand and interpret. Literally the results can be viewed in a 'tree' diagram which makes them a friendly way to show classification algorithm results.

In this lab, you'll use Orange to build and evaluate a decision tree that classifies real estate listings as either a house or a condo. You'll walk through steps to load the data, visualize it, split it into training and testing sets, and assess model performance using predictions and a confusion matrix.

9.1 Lesson Steps

Step 1: Load Data

Start a new workflow in Orange. From the Data menu, add a CSV File Import widget. Upload the file tutorial_dTree_house.csv.

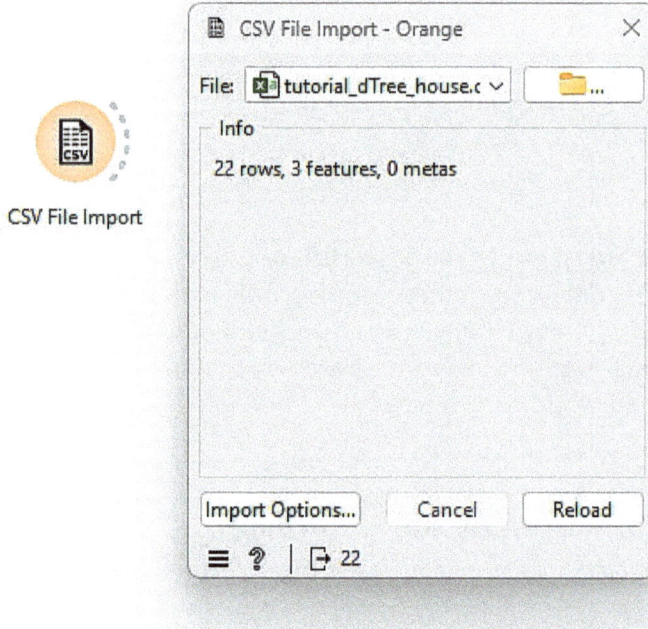

This dataset contains real estate listings, including price and square footage, along with the property type (house or condo). This will be used to train a decision tree classifier.

Step 2: Set Import Options

Double-click the CSV File Import widget. Click Import Options and set the data types to match the dataset—make sure categorical and numeric types are correctly identified.

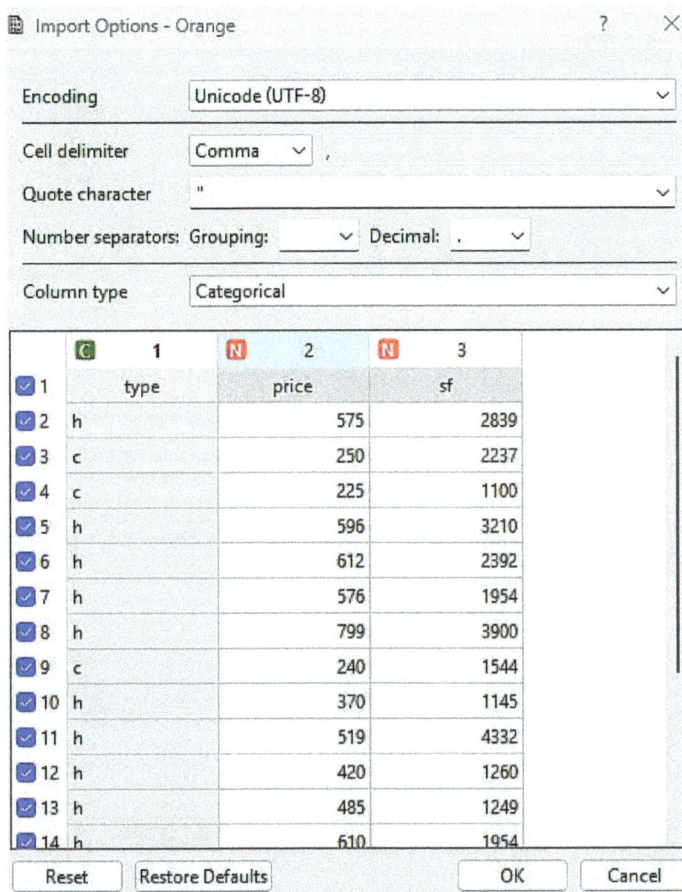

While decision trees do not require normalized data, correct data type assignment is still crucial for proper model training. Numeric features like price and square footage must be set correctly.

Step 3: Select Columns

From the Transform menu, add a Select Columns widget. Connect it to the CSV File Import widget.

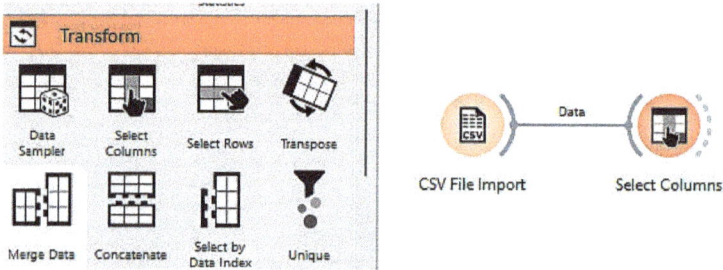

Double-click the widget and set 'features' (independent) and 'target' (dependent) variables. The target variable here is whether the real estate is a house or condo based on the features of price and square footage.

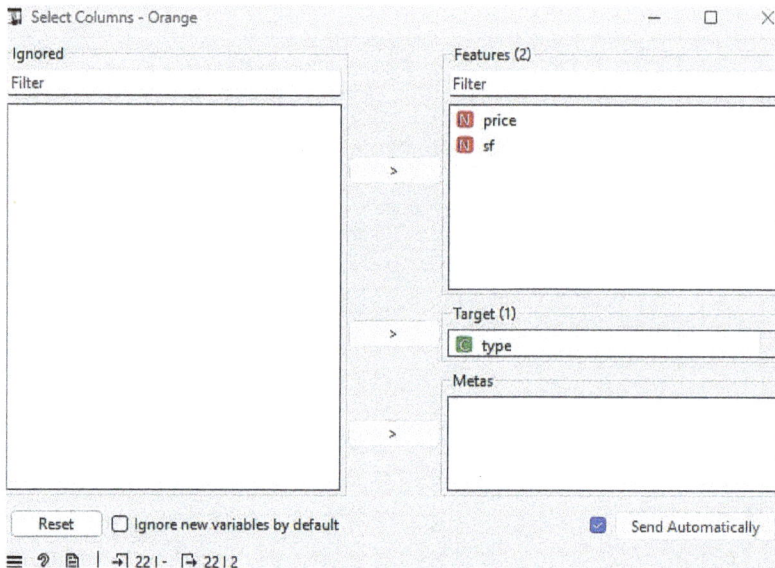

The model will use price and square footage to classify each listing as a house or a condo.

Step 4: Visualize with Scatter Plot

From the Visualize menu, add a Scatter Plot widget. Connect it to the Select Columns widget. Do a scatterplot of sf by price and color code it by type. Look at the scatterplot

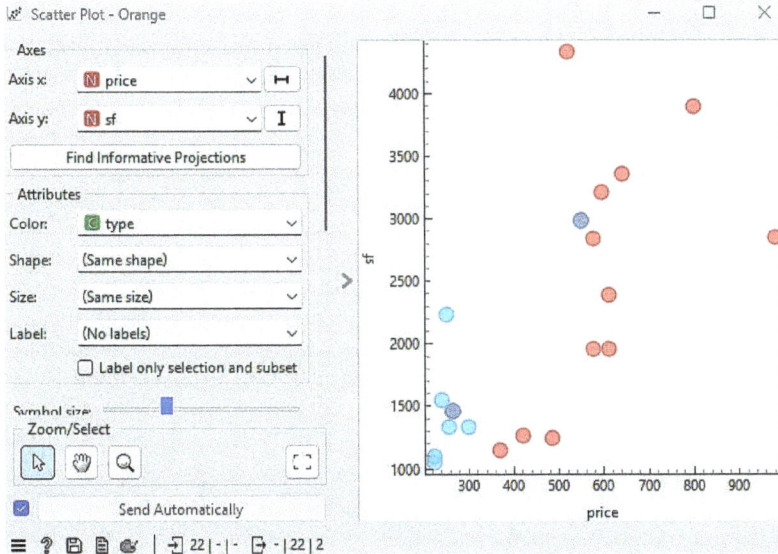

This gives you a quick visual of how the two features relate to the target variable. There is good separation in this data making it a great candidate for a decision tree.

Step 5: Split the Data

From the Transform menu, add a Data Sampler widget. Connect it to the Select Columns widget.

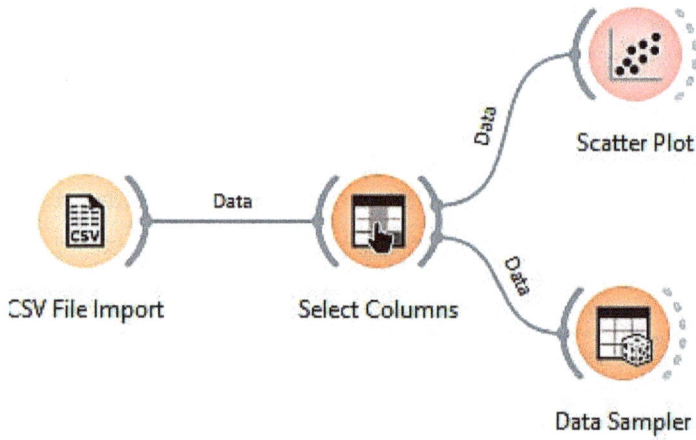

Double-click the Sample Data widget and set training percentage to 80%. Click the Sample Data button before closing.

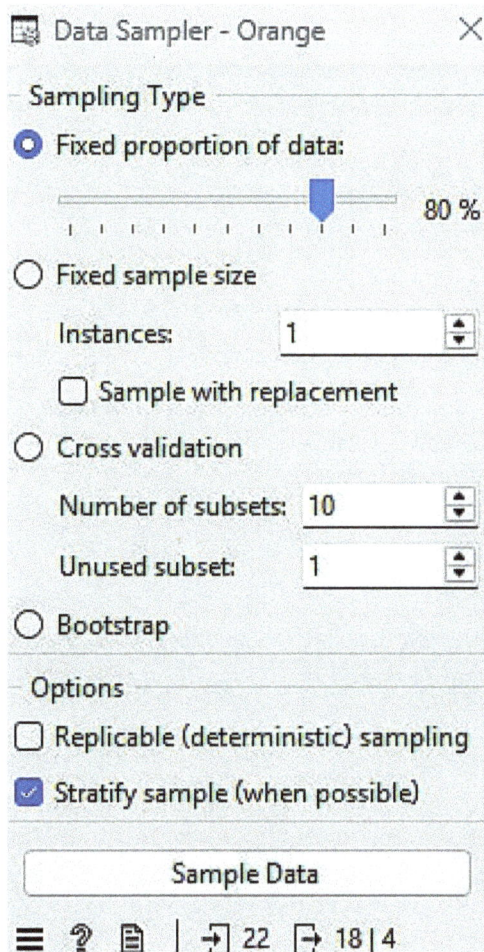

Splitting the data into training and testing sets allows you to evaluate how well your model generalizes to new, unseen data. Sampling ensures the model is trained only on part of the data.

Step 6: Add the Decision Tree Model

From the Model menu, add a Tree widget. From the Visualize menu, add a Tree Viewer widget. Connect the Tree widget to the training output of the Sample Data widget. Connect the Tree widget to the Tree Viewer.

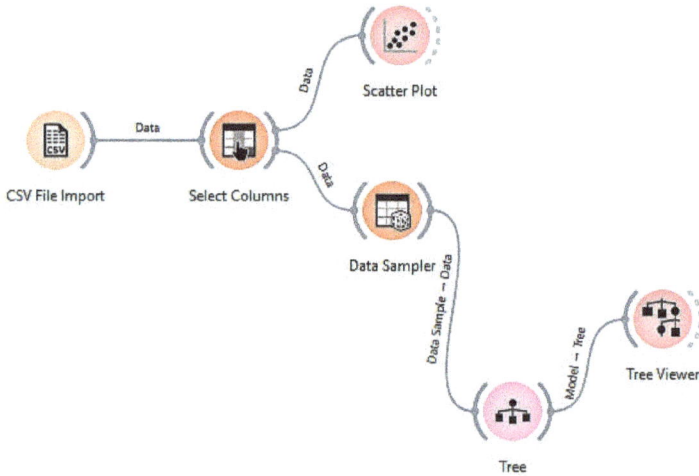

The Tree widget builds the model using the training data. The Tree Viewer
visualizes how decisions are made.

Step 7: View the Tree

Double-click the Tree Viewer widget. Open the Tree Viewer to see the decision tree built on the training data - note results will vary as this is based on
sampling. Set depth to two levels to look at the first split (realistically for a
dataset this small two levels is a good depth, but the full tree can be viewed
by increasing the depth).

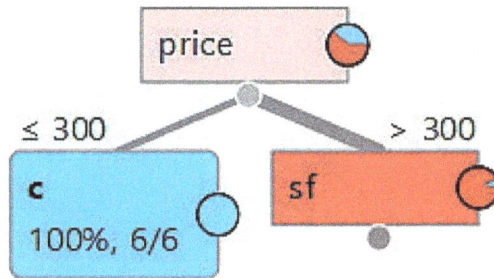

This is a sample result that shows the first split based on price (<300 is classi-fied as a condo and above 300 as a house).

Because the decision tree is based on sampling RESULTS WILL VARY. To test this after making a tree go back in the workflow and re-click 'sample data' and you may (not necessarily as it possible samples will yield same results) get a different result

Step 8: Evaluate the Model

From the Evaluate menu, add a Predictions widget and a Confusion Matrix widget. Connect the Tree to the Predictions widget (using training data). Con-nect the test output from the Sample Data widget to the Predictions widget. Then connect Predictions to Confusion Matrix.

Make sure all connectors show the same as depicted.

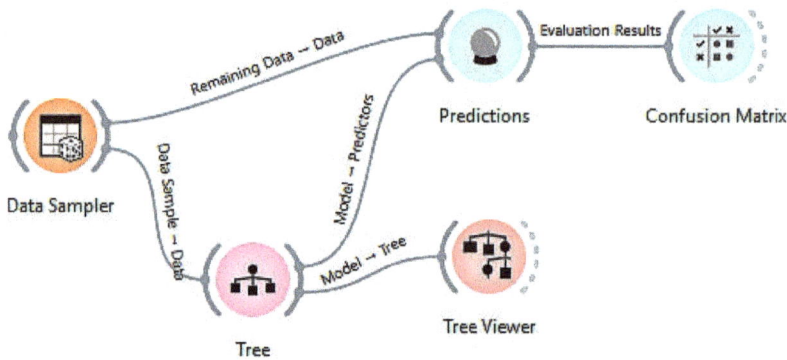

This workflow structure allows you to compare the model's predictions (on the test data) with the actual labels. It helps assess model accuracy and identify misclassifications.

Step 9: View the Confusion Matrix

Double-click the Confusion Matrix widget to view results.

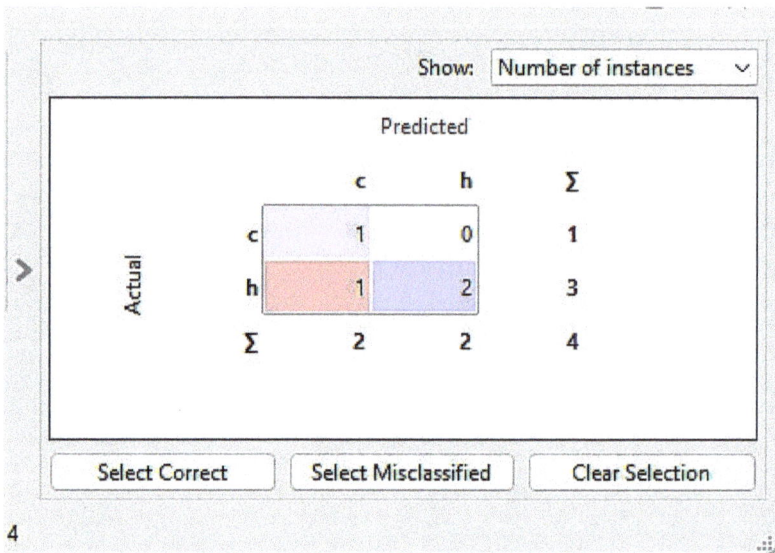

The matrix shows how many examples were correctly or incorrectly classified. Misclassifications can point to patterns the model struggled with, helping you refine the features or sample strategy. For this sample there is one misclassification (of a house misclassified as a condo). Reminder again: Because of random sampling, results may vary each time you click the Sample Data button. This randomness simulates real-world variability in training/testing splits.

9.2 Wrap-Up

This lab walked you through building a decision tree model from start to finish. You explored how real estate features like price and square footage can be used to predict property type, and you visualized the decision rules the model created. By splitting your data into training and test sets, you were able to evaluate how well the model performs on unseen data. The confusion matrix helped highlight any misclassifications, giving you insight into the model's strengths and limitations. Overall, this exercise showed how decision trees can serve as an intuitive and practical tool for classification tasks.

9.3   Exercises

Decision Trees

1. Begin a new workflow and add a CSV File Import widget. Load your dataset and verify that the data types are correctly set—numeric for numerical features and categorical for class labels.

2. Add a Select Columns widget to specify which columns will be used as features (independent variables) and which column is the target (dependent variable). Set any irrelevant columns to be ignored.

3. (Optional) Include a Scatter Plot or other visualization widget to examine the relationships between your features and the target variable.

4. Add a Sample Data widget to split your dataset into training and testing sets, typically using an 80/20 or 70/30 split (small data).

5. Insert a Tree widget connected to the training data output of the Sample Data widget. Add a Tree Viewer widget to visualize the resulting decision tree.

6. Add a Predictions widget, connecting it to both the Tree widget and the testing data output. Then add a Confusion Matrix widget connected to the Predictions widget to assess the model's classification performance.

Dataset 1: Real Estate Listing Classifier

Use the file real_estate_listings.csv. This dataset contains housing prices and square footage, with a label identifying whether the listing is a "House" or "Condo".

1. What feature is most used as the root node in your decision tree?
2. In the scatter plot, how do House and Condo listings cluster based on Price and SqFt?
3. What is the training/testing split used in this lab?
4. How many listings were misclassified in your confusion matrix?
5. What happens when you re-click the Sample Data widget—does the tree or accuracy change?

Dataset 2: Customer Churn Predictor

Use the file customer_churn.csv. This data includes monthly charges and customer tenure, with a binary target variable indicating whether a customer has churned (Yes/No).

6. Which feature—Monthly Charges or Tenure—was more important in predicting churn?
7. What was the first decision split in your tree for this dataset?
8. Did the tree misclassify any customers in the test set?
9. How does increasing training percentage (e.g., from 80% to 90%) affect accuracy?
10. Why might decision trees be preferred over logistic regression in this case?

Lab 10

Nearest Neighbors Classification (KNN)

The k-nearest neighbors (kNN) algorithm is a straightforward yet effective method for classification tasks. It makes predictions by comparing a data point to its closest neighbors (as measured by mathematical distance) in the training set.

In this lab, you'll use Orange to build a kNN model that predicts pant size based on height and weight. You'll learn how to prepare data through normalization, split it for training and testing, and evaluate how well the model performs. You'll also visualize both the raw and predicted data to understand the results more clearly.

_____

10.1   Lesson Steps

Step 1: Load Data

Start a new workflow in Orange. From the Data menu, add a CSV File Import widget. Upload the file tutorial_KNN_pants.csv.

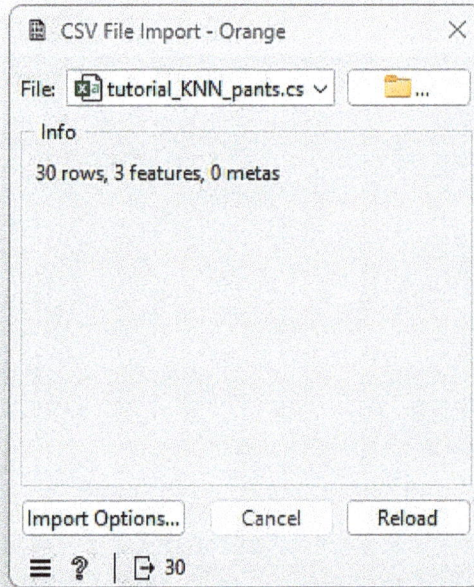

This dataset contains information for a classification task—predicting a category based on numeric features. It's used to demonstrate how the kNN algorithm works in Orange.

Step 2: Set Import Options

Double-click the CSV File Import widget. Click Import Options and ensure the data types are set correctly for each column.

kNN uses numeric values to calculate distances between data points. Properly assigning numeric types is essential for accurate distance calculations.

Step 3: Normalize the Data

From the Transform menu, add a Preprocess widget. Connect it to the CSV File Import widget.

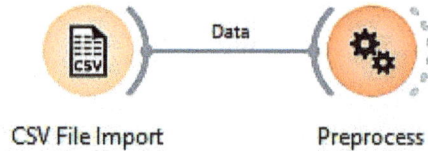

Double-click the Preprocess widget and choose Normalize Features > Standardize.

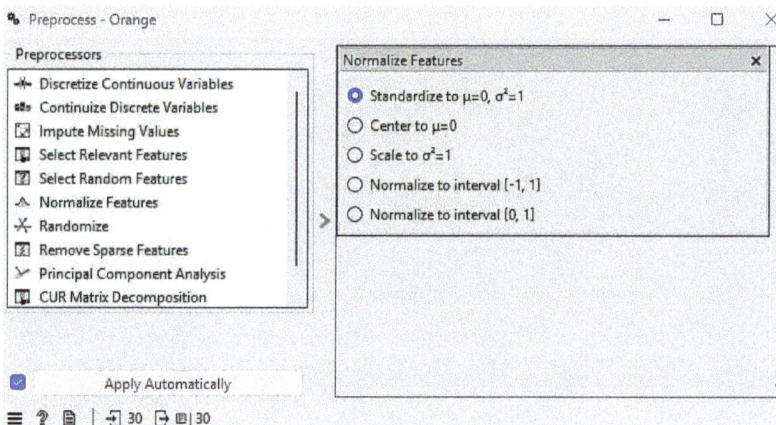

kNN relies on distance. If features are on different scales (e.g., weight in kg, height in cm), those with larger scales will dominate. Standardization (z-scores) solves this.

Step 4: View Normalized Data

From the Data menu, add a Data Table widget. Connect it to the Preprocess widget. Double-click to view the normalized data.

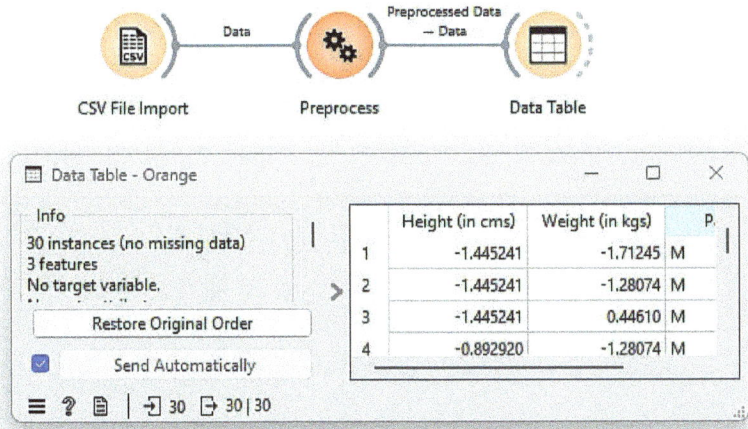

This allows you to confirm the normalization worked. The numeric values should now be centered around 0 with standard deviations of **Step 5: Set Up**

Columns for Modeling

From the Transform menu, add a Select Columns widget. Connect it to the Preprocess widget.

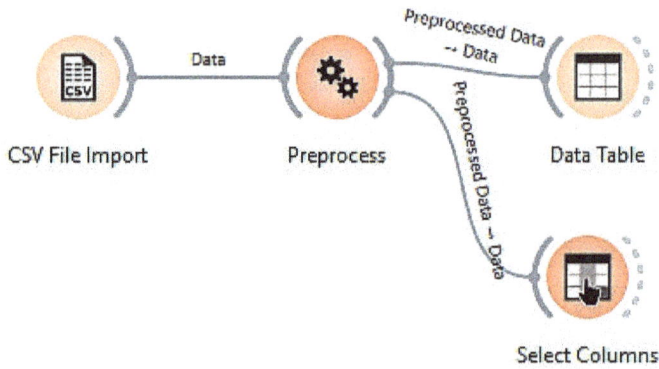

Double-click the widget to open it. Then, select the target variable, which is the one you want to predict—in this case, pant size. Next, choose the features, which are the independent variables used for making the prediction; here, those are height and weight.

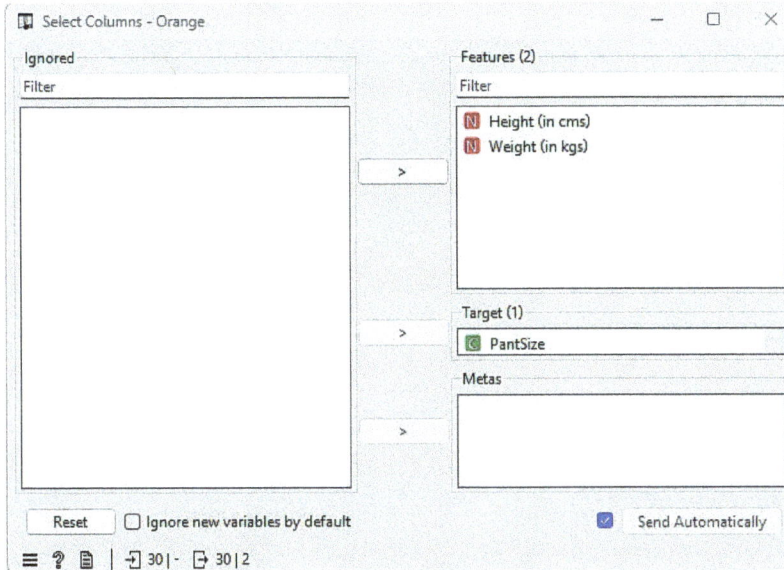

This step defines the inputs (features) and outputs (target) of your classification model.

Step 6: Sample the Data

Add a Data Sampler widget from the Transform menu. Connect it to the Select Columns widget.

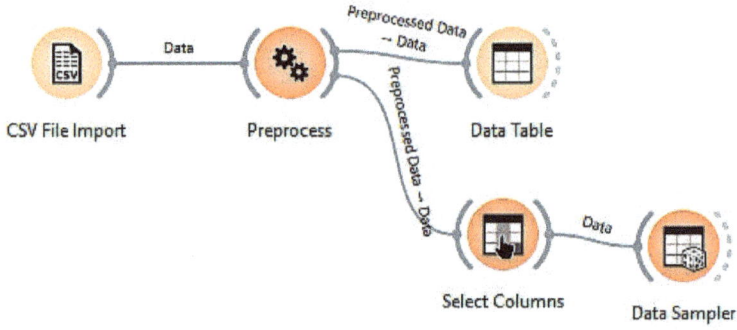

Double-click and set the Sample Percentage to 80%. Click Sample Data to generate the split.

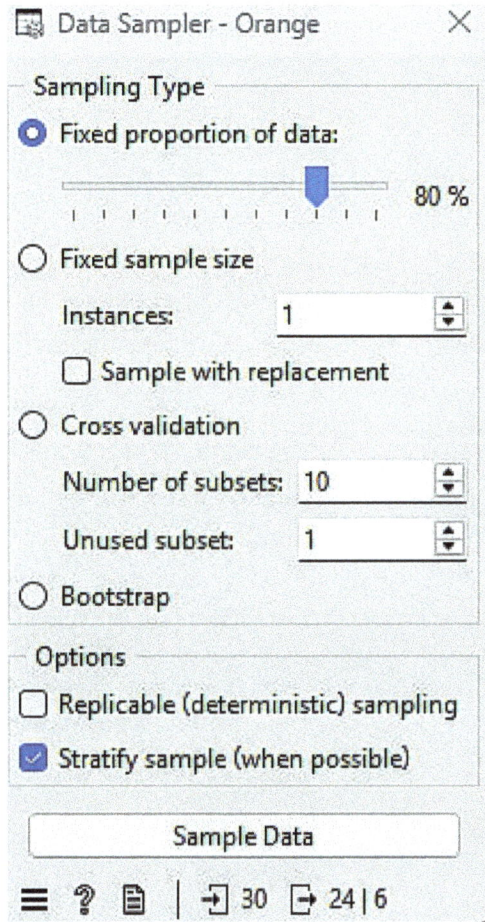

80% of the data will be used to train the model, while the remaining 20% will be used to test and evaluate its performance.

Step 7: Add kNN and Predictions Widgets

From the Model menu, add a kNN widget. From the Evaluate menu, add a Predictions widget. Click on the connector and set the data connector from the data sampler to kNN and set it as shown (to send the training data to kNN, it should say "Data Sampler - Data"). Click on the connector from the data sampler to the predictions widget and set it as shown (the test data does NOT go through kNN but flows directly to the predictions widget, it should say "Reaming Data - Data").

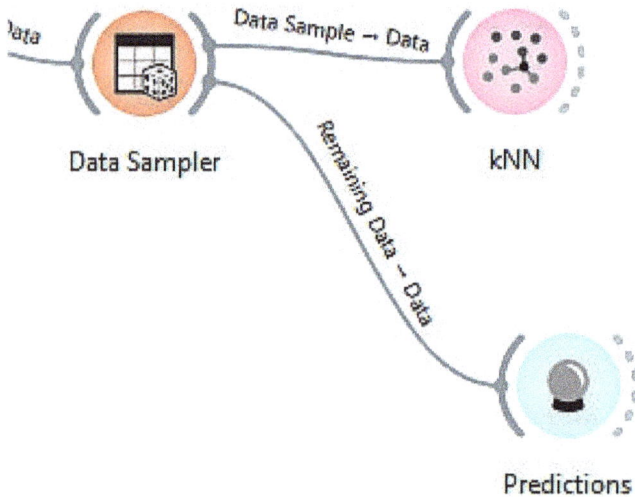

Note you may need to hit the "Clear All" button on the connector to set it correctly. This setup allows the model to be trained on 80% of the data, then used to make predictions on the 20% test set. It's important that the test data goes directly to the Predictions widget—not through the kNN model.

Step 8: Set the Number of Neighbors (k)

Double-click the kNN widget. Set k = 3.

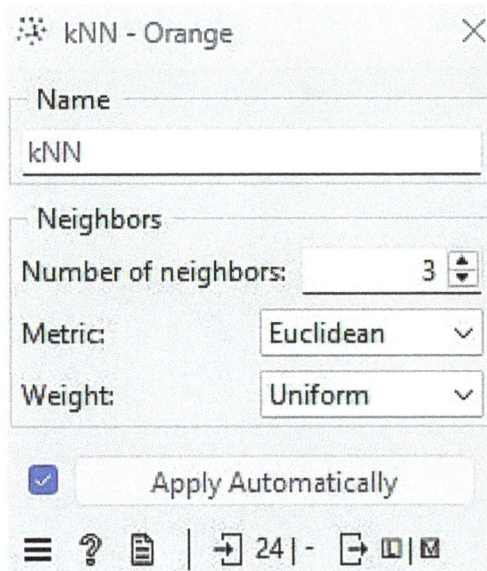

In k-nearest neighbors (kNN), k is a number that tells the algorithm how many nearby data points (neighbors) it should look at when making a prediction. When k = 3, the model will find the three closest points to a new data point and predict the label (like pant size) based on the majority vote from those three neighbors. So, k controls how many comparisons the model makes to decide what category the new data belongs to.

Choosing k = 3 in k-nearest neighbors (kNN) is common because it offers a simple, balanced starting point. If you set k = 1, the prediction depends only on the closest neighbor, which makes the model very sensitive to noise or unusual points. On the other hand, if k is too large (like 10), the model may include too many faraway points that don't really match the test case, which can blur the differences between categories. The value used for k is always odd since an even k would result in ties.

Step 9: Setup to Get Results

Add a connector from kNN to predictions and adjust it so it has "Model - Predictions" on the connector (this will send the predicted values from the training data).

From the Evaluate menu, add a Confusion Matrix widget. Connect the Predictions widget to the Confusion Matrix.

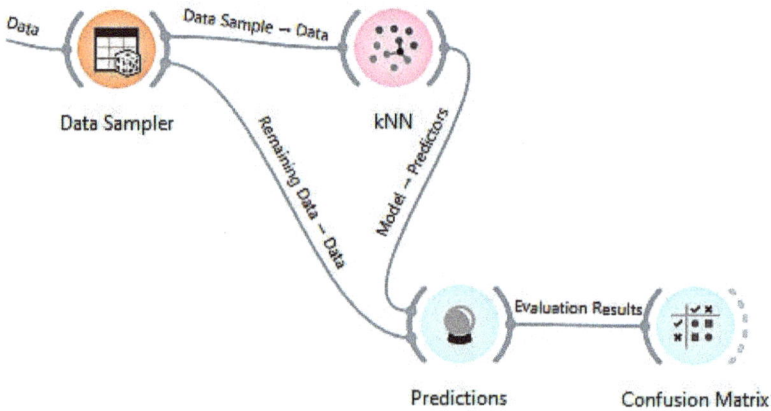

This matrix shows how many predictions were correct or incorrect, giving you a quick performance summary of the model.

Step 10: View the Results

Double-click the Predictions widget to view the output. This will show the (on the left) predicted classes aligned with the data. This sample (results will vary) shows no misclassifications.

Also look at the confusion matrix which is a table of predicted vs. actual values and a matrix showing how many instances were classified correctly or incorrectly. There are no incorrect classifications in this sample.

Note: Results may vary because sampling introduces randomness.

Step 11: Visualize with Scatter Plot

From the Visualize menu, add a Scatter Plot widget. Connect it to both the

Select Columns widget and the Predictions widget.

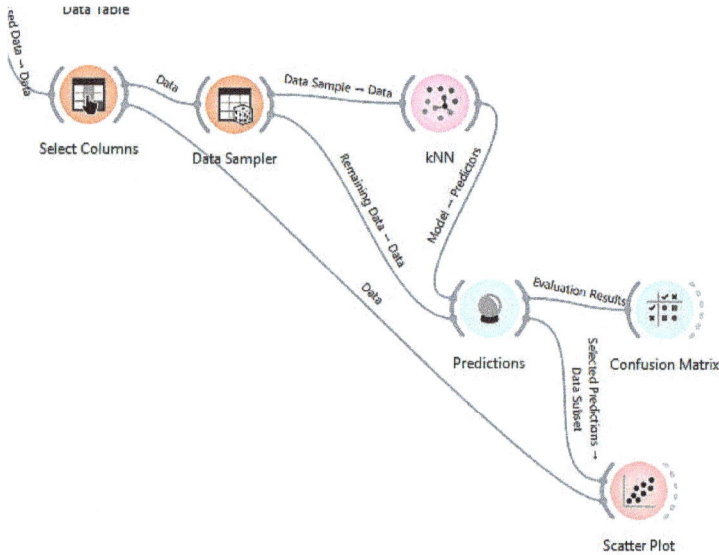

The scatter plot will show both raw data and predicted classifications. This is helpful to trace how different points were classified and why misclassifications may have occurred. This scatterplot has no misclassifications (testing samples in filled dots, there are 6 testing samples but one of the data is the same measures and a double point) but if there were misclassifications they can be visually traced on the plot.

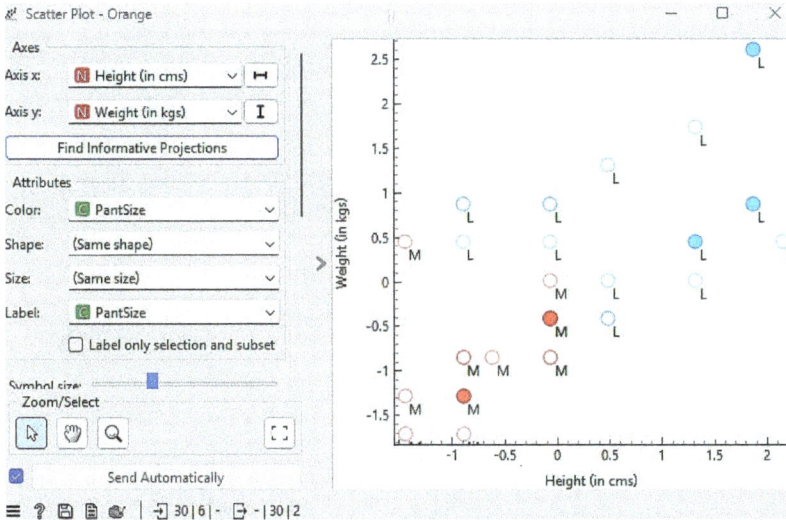

10.2 Wrap-Up

This lab gave you hands-on experience with nearest neighbors classification. You started by normalizing the data to ensure fair distance calculations, then built and tested a kNN model using height and weight to predict pant size. With visualizations and a confusion matrix, you were able to interpret model accuracy and explore how predictions matched the actual outcomes. Overall, kNN provides a powerful but intuitive approach to classification, especially when patterns in the data are local and clearly defined.

10.3   Exercises

Nearest Neighbors Classification (KNN)

1. Import each CSV dataset into Orange.
2. Normalize features using the Preprocess widget.
3. Split the data using Data Sampler or Sample Data (80% training, 20% testing).
4. Build and evaluate a kNN model.
5. Answer all questions with text, output, or screenshots as applicable.

Dataset 1: knn_animals.csv

This dataset contains numeric features weight (kg) and height (cm) for animals, with the target variable animal_type.

1. Show the first 5 rows of normalized weight and height after preprocessing.
2. Which column did you assign as the target variable?
3. What value of k did you select and why?
4. Provide the confusion matrix results after running the model on the test data.
5. What is the overall accuracy or error rate from your confusion matrix?

Dataset 2: knn_customers.csv

This dataset has numeric features purchase_frequency and avg_spent with categorical loyalty_status.

6. After normalization, show the summary statistics or first few rows of features purchase_frequency and avg_spent.
7. Which feature columns and target did you assign?
8. What happens if you change k from 3 to 7? Explain briefly.
9. Provide the confusion matrix output for your model predictions. How many samples were misclassified?
10. Create a scatter plot of purchase_frequency vs avg_spent colored by predicted loyalty_status and describe what you observe.

Lab 11

Association Analysis

Association analysis helps uncover relationships between items that appear together (or associate) in datasets like shopping baskets or transaction records. In this lab, you'll explore these kinds of patterns identifying common item combinations, and generating if-then rules that describe how one item may suggest the presence of another.

Association analysis is a very common and important analytical technique for optimizing many business processes in retail and other applications as well as has medical uses and implications (disease and symptom associations, drug reactions).

11.1   Lesson Steps

Step 1: Start Workflow and Load Data

Start a new Orange workflow. From the Data menu, add a CSV File Import widget. Load the file: tutorial_twoItemBasket.csv.

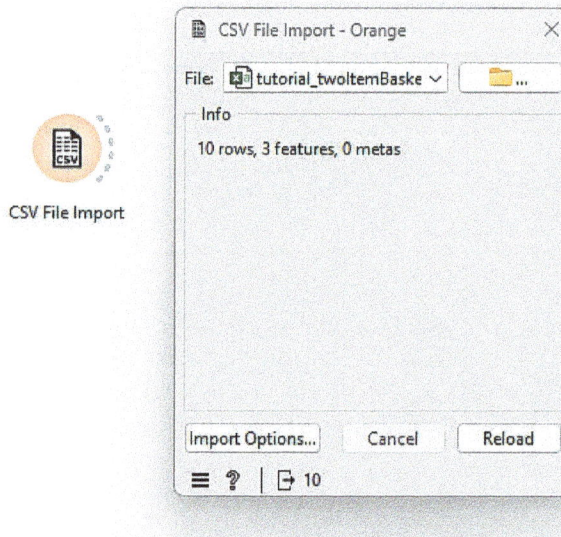

CSV File Import

Important. The setup of the import dataset should have one column per item (e.g., columns for Pen, Paper, Ink). Each column contains 1 if the item is present in that transaction. Do not fill in zeros. An optional Transaction ID column can be present but is not required.

A	B	C	D
Transaction	Milk	Butter	
1	1		
2	1		
3		1	
4		1	
5	1	1	
6		1	
7	1		
8	1	1	
9			
10		1	

Association analysis in Orange is designed for market basket-type data, where each transaction records the presence of specific items. Zeros are unnecessary and may confuse the model. You may need to work with and restructure your data before importing it in Orange.

Step 2: Set Data Types

Double-click the CSV File Import widget. Click Import Options. Set each item column (with 1s) to Categorical. Set the Transaction ID column (if present) to Ignore.

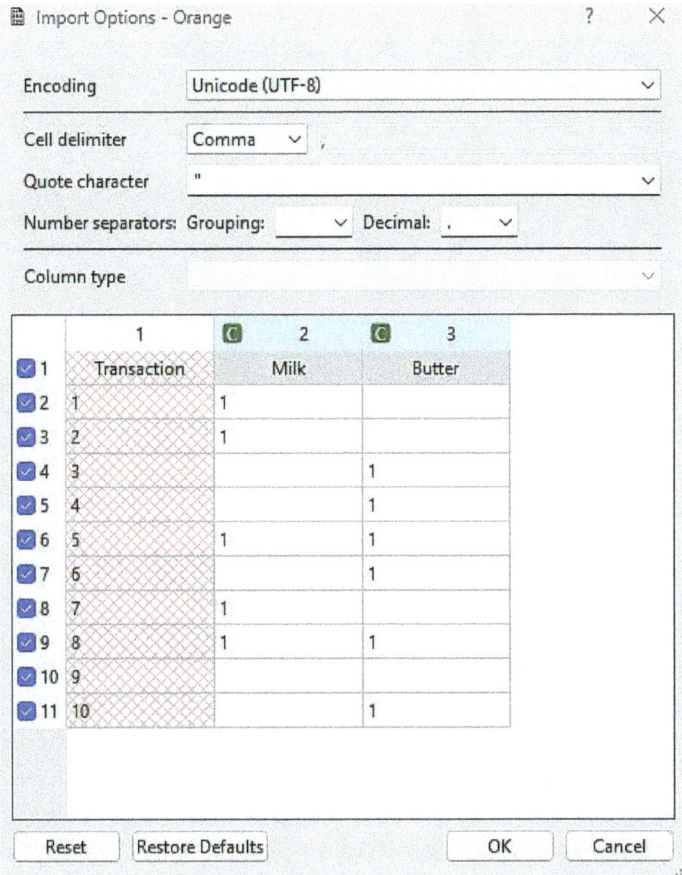

Orange treats binary item indicators as categorical data for association rule mining. Setting data types ensures proper interpretation of inputs during pattern discovery.

Step 3: Add Frequent Itemsets Widget

Note: If the Associate menu is missing, go to Options > Add-ons and install the Associate add-on. This may not have been installed as part of the default options when Orange was first installed (Orange has numerous add on packages).

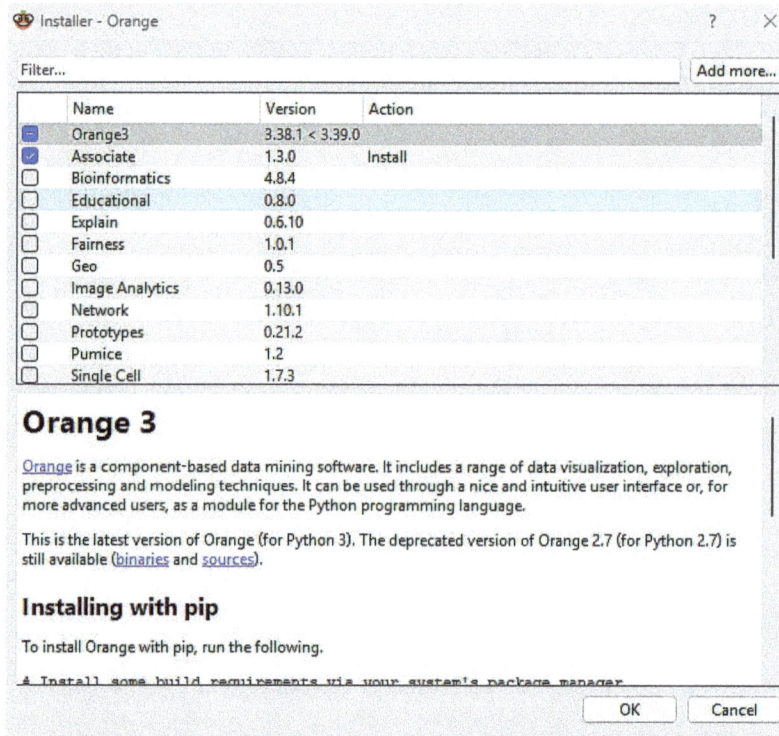

From the Associate menu, add a Frequent Itemsets widget. Connect it to the CSV File Import widget.

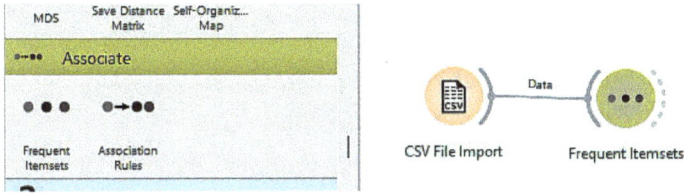

This widget identifies sets of items that frequently appear together in transactions. It's the first step in discovering associations in the data.

Step 4: Explore Frequent Itemsets

Open the Frequent Itemsets widget. Set Minimal support to the lowest level and check boxes as shown below.

Click to expand itemsets of different sizes (1-item, 2-item, etc.).

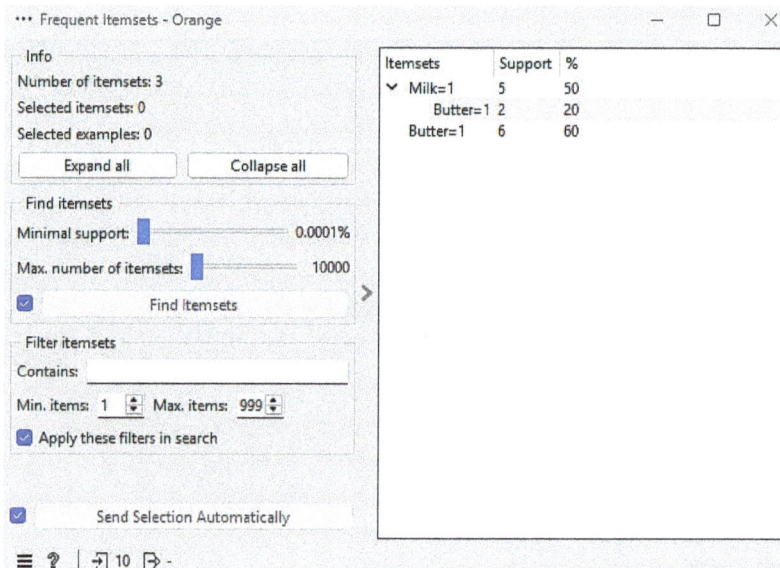

Review support values for each itemset. Support measures how frequently an itemset appears across all transactions. Use filters (optional) to narrow down to itemsets with high or low support.

Step 5: Add Association Rules Widget

From the Associate menu, add an Association Rules widget. Connect it to the same input data.

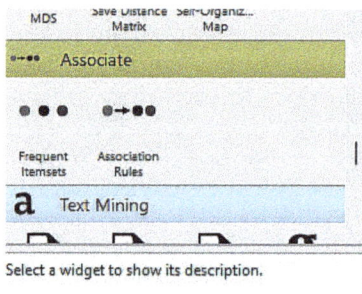

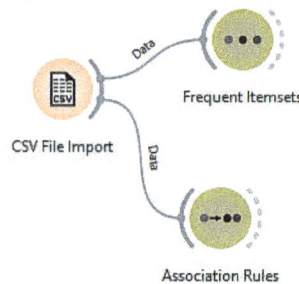

This widget generates if-then rules like Pen ⊘ Paper, showing how the presence of one item implies the presence of another.

Step 6: Find and View Association Rules

Open the Association Rules widget. Click the Find Rules button to display rules. Adjust support, confidence, or lift thresholds and explore what is displayed (set them all to the lowest levels).

This step generates rules using the thresholds you set for support, confidence, and lift. Support tells you how often the items in the rule appear together in the dataset. Confidence shows how likely the second item (the result) is to appear when the first item (the condition) is present. Lift compares the likelihood of the result happening with the condition to how often it would happen by chance, helping you judge the strength of the rule. These values help identify which rules are worth paying attention to.

Step 7: Save Association Rules (Optional)

Add a Data Table widget. Connect it to the Association Rules widget. Adjust the connection to output Rules (click the connector line to change the data type). Add a Save Data widget to export as a .csv file. Click on Save to direct where the file is saved.

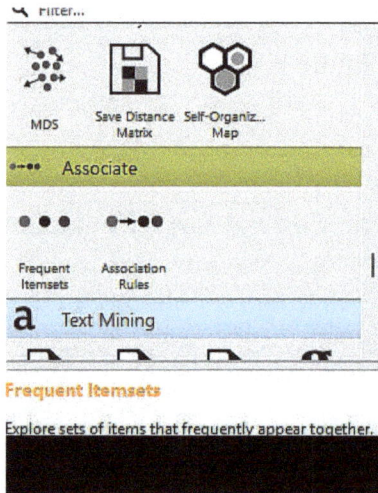

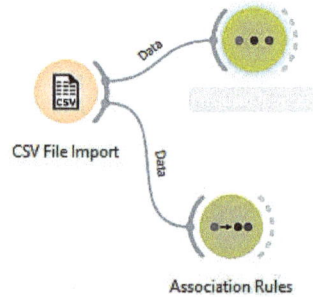

11.2   Wrap-Up

This lab walked through how to carry out association analysis using Orange, from preparing the data to viewing and exporting the rules. You used the Frequent Itemsets widget to find common groupings and the Association Rules widget to build meaningful if-then statements. By adjusting support, confidence, and lift values, you learned how to control which rules are shown and how to decide which ones are most useful. This type of analysis is especially valuable in market research, recommendation systems, and behavioral insights.

11.3 Exercises

Association Analysis

1. Import each dataset into Orange using the CSV File Import widget.
2. Set all item columns to categorical and ignore any ID columns if present.
3. Use the Frequent Itemsets widget to find frequent itemsets with user-defined minimum support thresholds.
4. Use the Association Rules widget to generate and explore rules by adjusting support, confidence, and lift thresholds.
5. Answer all questions with textual explanations or screenshots of outputs (frequent itemsets, rules, confusion matrix, etc.).
6. Optionally save rules using Data Table and Save Data widgets.

Dataset 1: basket_office.csv

This dataset records 20 transactions of office supply items. Each column corresponds to an item; a '1' indicates the item was bought in that transaction. No zeros are recorded.

1. How many 1-item frequent itemsets are found with support ≥ 0.3? List them.
2. Identify any 2-item frequent itemsets with support ≥ 0.3.
3. Provide 3 association rules with confidence ≥ 0.7 and list their support, confidence, and lift.
4. Which item(s) appear most frequently across all transactions?
5. Explain in your own words what lift means and identify a rule with lift > 1 from your results.

Dataset 2: basket_grocery.csv

This dataset records 20 grocery shopping transactions.

6. How many frequent 1-itemsets have support ≥ 0.35? List them.
7. List any 2-itemsets with support ≥ 0.3.
8. Provide 3 association rules with confidence ≥ 0.75. Include support, confidence, and lift values.
9. Which items frequently appear together? Describe any interesting patterns you observe.
10. Using the association rules, suggest one potential product placement or marketing strategy for the grocery store.

www.ingramcontent.com/pod-product-compliance
Lightning Source LLC
Chambersburg PA
CBHW051907210326
41597CB00033B/6056